Stars of the
New Jersey Shore

A Theatrical History

1860s-1930s

Karen L. Schnitzspahn

Schiffer Publishing Ltd

4880 Lower Valley Road Atglen, Pennsylvania 19310

Dedication

To my husband, Leon, *My Lucky Star* – with love

Published by Schiffer Publishing Ltd.
4880 Lower Valley Road
Atglen, PA 19310
Phone: (610) 593-1777; Fax: (610) 593-2002
E-mail: Info@schifferbooks.com

For the largest selection of fine reference books on this and related subjects, please visit
our web site at **www.schifferbooks.com**
We are always looking for people to write books on new and related subjects. If you have
an idea for a book please contact us at the above address.

This book may be purchased from the publisher.
Include $3.95 for shipping.
Please try your bookstore first.
You may write for a free catalog.

In Europe, Schiffer books are distributed by
Bushwood Books
6 Marksbury Ave.
Kew Gardens
Surrey TW9 4JF England
Phone: 44 (0) 20 8392-8585; Fax: 44 (0) 20 8392-9876
E-mail: info@bushwoodbooks.co.uk
Website: www.bushwoodbooks.co.uk

All illustrations in this book are from the author's personal collection of photographs, postcards, and other memorabilia, unless otherwise credited.

Designed by Mark David Bowyer
Type set in Seagull Hv BT / Aldine721 BT

ISBN: 978-0-7643-2719-3
Printed in China

Contents

Acknowledgments

The research for this book has been ongoing for almost twenty years, so I am indebted to many people. Their names could probably fill a whole book! I'll acknowledge some of the most significant ones here, but thank you to everyone who has contributed information and provided encouragement.

My deepest appreciation goes to esteemed historian and author, George H. Moss Jr. He is my colleague and friend, who encouraged me to preserve theatrical history and wrote the Foreword to this work. I am grateful to Art Scott, a fine writer and aficionado of popular culture, for his assistance and friendship. I am indebted to Randall Gabrielan, an outstanding New Jersey author and historian, who knows the value of sharing historical information. Special thanks goes to Kathy Dorn Severini, of Dorn's Classic Images, who keeps up the family tradition of preserving and providing historic images of Monmouth County. Thanks are in store for my good friend, Sandra Epstein, co-author of a previous work with me and a fellow "history detective." I'd like to express my gratitude to the Mantell family group, especially Laurie Sisson for all her kindness. My sincere thanks goes to the distinguished author, Robert Pinsky, for allowing me to quote from his work. Thank you also Rick Benjamin, director of the Paragon Ragtime Orchestra, who keeps yesteryear's music alive. I am grateful to Carolyn Crawford for sharing her exceptional knowledge of "E.B." Thank you to Red Bank artist Evelyn Leavens, and to Bill Zervas.

During the course of this work, I have visited and contacted scores of libraries and museums. Many professionals from these institutions have helped, and I am grateful to them all. I would especially like to thank Raymond Wemmlinger, Curator and Librarian of the Hampden-Booth Theatre Library, New York, for his assistance with my on-going interest in theatrical history. Thank you to the staff members of The New York Public Library at Lincoln Center. A special thank you goes to Janet Birckhead, of the Long Branch Free Public Library, whose dedication to the local collections is outstanding. Jane Eigenrauch, of The Red Bank Public Library, is always willing to help and I greatly appreciate her. Thanks also to Chris Ellwood, Manager of Special Collections of the Murry and Leonie Guggenheim Memorial Library at Monmouth University, Mary Ann Kiernan of The

Monmouth County Archives, Carla Tobias of The Monmouth County Historical Association's library, and the reference staff of the Monmouth County Library, Eastern Branch.

Many fine organizations with dedicated volunteers work to preserve the history of Monmouth County. They deserve thanks for all the worthwhile things they do. I would like to mention a few that have been particularly helpful with this project: The Atlantic Highlands Historical Society, The Long Branch Historical Association, The Ocean Township Historical Museum, and The Monmouth County Historical Association.

During the creation of this book, several significant people have passed away. I would like to recognize these individuals. Peggy Hollingsworth and Fran Musone - both lovely people who contributed greatly to my research and encouraged my interest in Robert B. Mantell. Also, talented author Karen Plunkett-Powell; though not directly involved with this book, gave me incentive to write.

I pay tribute to Timothy J. McMahon, who was an excellent historian and author. He took a special interest in the theatrical history of Red Bank and Fair Haven, where he lived in a small house that he said once belonged to a vaudevillian—a tightrope walker! It was a privilege to know Tim, a treat to read his articles in The Two River Times, and great fun to hear his lively accounts of local history. He is missed by all.

Going back to the present, I am grateful to Tina Skinner of Schiffer Publishing for her guidance and for believing in my work.

Last, but of course not least, I express my appreciation and love for my family, who are always my inspiration: Leon, Doug, Radha, Isa, Kieran, Greg (aka Max), and Erin, too. Oh, and thank you to our elderly cat, Cleo, for sitting faithfully beside me as I write.

Foreword

"There is no business like show business" is a phrase that has been heard for years. This incredible new book, Stars of the New Jersey Shore, provides details of a particular portion of show business history.

The author, Karen L. Schnitzspahn, has had a longtime interest in the theater and Monmouth County. She is a writer and historian well known for her many regional books and articles. As a result of her years of dedicated research, this particular work is a classic history of the Monmouth County shore and its relationship with many theatrical people who made it their home.

Although the focus is on the performers, this book also includes information about the theatrical venues of the past at the Monmouth County shore. In their day, Asbury Park, Red Bank, and Long Branch offered a full range of theater (both professional and amateur) including vaudeville, musical comedy, drama, opera, and burlesque. Live entertainment was found in theaters, rented halls, auditoriums, and even on a floating stage!

The more than a hundred illustrations included in this publication are a treasure; they add so much to the individual biographies. After reading about the players and seeing their images, you will really feel as though you know them. Maggie Mitchell, Edwin Booth, Lillie Langtry, and Lillian Russell are no longer merely names in a text!

You may meet some performers you never even heard of before, long forgotten though famous in their day, and find their stories to be fascinating. We can be grateful to Karen Schnitzspahn for sharing her knowledge and love of this subject with her readers and for presenting a unique look at our cultural heritage.

Now, "on with the show!"

—George H. Moss Jr.
Official Historian of Monmouth County, New Jersey

An observer and picture historian of the New Jersey shore for over sixty years, George H. Moss Jr. is the author of numerous books and articles on subjects ranging from local history to antique automobiles and early recordings of the American theater. He has received numerous awards of recognition for his continuing preservation of New Jersey's history. Karen Schnitzspahn had the pleasure of being his co-author for two books: *Those Innocent Years: 1898-1914, Images of the Jersey Shore from the Pach Photographic Collection* and *Victorian Summers at the Grand Hotels of Long Branch*.

Preface

My enthusiasm for theatrical history began when I would leaf through my grandmother's copy of Daniel Blum's *Great Stars of the American Stage, A Pictorial Record.* That was in the 1950s, while I was growing up in central New Jersey. As a grammar school kid, I sported a ponytail, poodle skirt, saddle shoes, and bobby sox. Naturally, Elvis, the Mouseketeers, and Sandra Dee were high on my list of favorite stars, but something about those performers of earlier times in the book intrigued me. The exaggerated expressions on their faces and the details of their costumes were appealing. When I'd ask my Grandma about the actors in the book, she'd reply with something like, "Oh, my goodness, you never heard of Lillian Russell? She was a *real* star!"

One day, in the early 1980s, I took the old Daniel Blum pictorial that was once my Grandma's out of our bookcase and read that the great tragedian, Robert B. Mantell, had a "farm" in Atlantic Highlands. I began to wonder how many other stars of yesteryear once lived in my area of the New Jersey shore. Then, while working on publications about local history, I found many references to the great actors who summered in Long Branch, Red Bank, Asbury Park, and other New Jersey shore resorts.

Serendipitously, in the late 1980s, an item I spotted at the preview for an auction would influence my life evermore. Up for bids was a brown cardboard "beer" box that contained several hundred slightly warped nineteenth century theatrical cabinet photos. Tossed in with many unfamiliar faces, there were pictures of Edwin Booth, Maggie Mitchell, Lillian Russell, Lillie Langtry, and the Barrymores. There were a few other bidders, but I knew that I simply had to have those photos! I held my number card up high. When the auctioneer's gavel slammed down, I had won the box for a modest sum.

In the years since then, I have researched these performers and many others, some of them terribly forgotten. Now, I feel it is time to share my knowledge and passion for the stars who lived in the New Jersey shore communities of Monmouth County—long before Bruce Springsteen was even born!

Introduction

Focus on the Players

This book features vignettes about theatrical people who were significant to the Monmouth County, New Jersey shore, from the mid-1860s until around 1930. Hundreds, perhaps thousands, of performers visited or lived here during this time, from the close of the Civil War to the beginning of The Great Depression, when moving pictures became affordable entertainment.

In the second half of the nineteenth century, politicians, financiers, authors, artists, sports figures, musicians, and actors all flocked to the Jersey coast for rest and relaxation. Easily accessible from New York or Philadelphia, the shore area's scenery, cool breezes, healthy sea bathing, and delicious meals at hotels and restaurants attracted these visitors. Most of them came to vacation, but there were also famous athletes who would train and actors who would rehearse the coming season's repertoire. Some of the rich and famous came for the fashions and social life, some to gamble, and some of them wisely invested in real estate. Many of the visiting celebrities decided to make the area their home base and raise families here, others retired here, and for some the New Jersey shore became their final resting place.

Chapters ("Acts") cover some particular towns along the New Jersey coast of Monmouth County that had the greatest concentration of theatrical performers during the years covered in this book. A few areas included are not directly on the coast, but on a river or bay and within five miles or so of the Atlantic Ocean.

This work is by no means a town-by-town history of shore theaters or their architecture, although some theaters are described, when significant. Only a small number of theaters were built for live entertainment at the New Jersey shore in the early days, but lecture halls and auditoriums provided venues for performers. Many of the theaters built in the first few decades of the twentieth century were designed for both live vaudeville acts and movies. By the close of the 1930s, most new theaters were constructed exclusively to show films. There were dozens of great movie houses all along the New Jersey coast, but only a few of them remain today, and most of them are in jeopardy.

I have tried to be accurate, but previous sources may be in error. I have presented the facts, but some legends and scandals are also included. After all, juicy stories about "stars," whether at the Jersey shore of yesteryear or Hollywood today, are the stuff that most people want to read about! Tabloid-style publications have been around for a long time.

If you do not find one of your favorite old time stars, or your great aunt who was in vaudeville is not mentioned, please understand that it would be impossible to include every performer who came to the Monmouth County shore in one small book. I worked with the publications and illustrations that were available to me, no doubt more material will continue to become available. I hope you will enjoy taking a journey back in time to meet this cast of stars as much as I have.

Act I
Long Branch

The Lure of "The Branch"

"The stars who can afford it delight in sitting under their own vine and fig tree at least for a portion of the year. No class of people appreciates the word home so much as the wandering players. Tossed about from city to city for eight months out of the twelve, they learn to estimate home life at its true value. A cottage at Long Branch just fills the bill..." *Brooklyn Eagle*, July 10, 1881

The Rich and the Famous

It seemed that everyone who was anyone summered at Long Branch. The seaside resort rapidly became as fashionable as Newport and Saratoga, the leading nineteenth century destinations for the rich and famous in America. In 1861, soon after the official onset of The Civil War, first lady Mary Todd Lincoln paid a much-publicized visit to Long Branch and stayed at the Mansion House, an oceanfront hotel. The celebrated artist Winslow Homer visited Long Branch in the 1860s and his detailed engravings of the resort appeared as illustrations in *Harper's Weekly* and *Harper's Monthly* magazines.

The sandy bluffs along the Atlantic Ocean at Long Branch provide a natural dramatic setting for this c.1905 postcard. Grand hotels of "The American Brighton" that hosted the rich and famous once lined Ocean Avenue.

Statesmen, generals, financiers, entrepreneurs, authors, and actors found Long Branch to be an ideal place to vacation. Many of them would decide to rent or buy summer homes.

At the invitation of friends, President Ulysses S. Grant came to town with his family in 1869 and established his "summer white house" at the Elberon section of Long Branch. It was Grant's presence that truly put Long Branch on the map. Over the years, seven presidents would spend time at "The Branch" – Grant, Hayes, Garfield, Arthur, Benjamin Harrison, McKinley, and Wilson (at West Long Branch).

Photos of President Ulysses S. Grant's "Summer White House" at Elberon became popular souvenirs with visitors to Long Branch in the late 1860s.This is one of the views taken by Pach Brothers. The cottages of the actors' colony were mostly inland to the west of Grant's oceanfront cottage.

Place Your Bets

Perhaps even more enticing than sea bathing to some Victorians was the gambling that Long Branch offered. Casinos, known as gambling clubs, lured visitors to "The Branch" starting in the 1860s with Phil Daly's Pennsylvania Club being the most celebrated of them all. In order to compete with the popular resort of Saratoga, Long Branch needed a horse racing course. On July 30, 1870, Monmouth Park opened (original track was in nearby Eatontown) and became a major attraction. Women did not frequent the gambling clubs but were allowed at the track.

A Colony of Player Folk

By the mid-nineteenth century, theatrical people from metropolitan areas had discovered Long Branch, accessible from New York or Philadelphia, for their much-needed vacations. Big city theaters were not open during the heat of the summer, and actors who toured had little desire to travel far during their time off. Some of them wanted the excitement and luxury of the hotels, but it seems that many thespians longed simply to have some peace and quiet. The bohemian "player folk," as they were called, found solace in establishing a community of cottages close to one another. The area at the south end of Long Branch known as West End (after London's West End) and the less developed southwestern section of Elberon attracted the actors. They could enjoy the tranquility of a rural landscape with farms and open land only a mile or two from the beach. Many players purchased property in the area of West Long Branch that is now mostly Monmouth University and in today's residential area of Oakhurst in Ocean Township. The entire area was generally referred to as "Long Branch" in those days and the actors' colony thrived there until around 1900.

This stereograph of "The Race at Monmouth Park" is from the early 1870s. Nineteenth century actress and author, Olive Logan, described the scene at the racecourse in the September 1876 *Harper's New Monthly Magazine:*
"Fashion is a queer moralist; and the same people who would be horrified at the thought of joining the throng in Chamberlin's club-house to toy with its tiger go without a qualm to the races at Monmouth Park, and bet their money on the running of horses instead of on the turning of a card."

Learned Birds and Headless Men

When the actors first began to frequent the area, there were no theaters at Long Branch. Shows were presented at the hotels but these were usually light entertainment, not full length dramas. An 1872 poster for The Ocean Hotel announced the appearance of an illusionist accompanied by trained animals including learned birds, performing white mice, and a trained Russian cat! Also on the bill was "The Man with the Talking Hand," a ventriloquist who appeared with his "Headless Men."[1] More sophisticated entertainment was also presented to hotel guests including appearances by opera stars, musicales, and rousing band concerts.

Surf and Dudes

Long Branch, called "The American Brighton" after Great Britain's famed seaside resort, needed to compete with the activities offered at Newport and other American resorts. The play by actress and author Olive Logan called *Surf or Summer Scenes at Long Branch*, complete with "realistic" special effects of bathers jumping in the waves, made a big hit with New Yorkers in 1870.

A program for the 1870s musical comedy, *The Dudes at Long Branch*, provides fascinating details about the plot and characters of the popular show.

To conclude with an entirely new and original Musical Comedy, a satire on the latest New York fashion craze, entitled

The Dudes at Long Branch

Written by the talented Vocal Comedian, HARRY MONTAGUE. Illustrated in One Act and Five Scenes.

CHARACTERS.

ARTHUR HAVILAND, the dear boy, a regular Dude of the period, his first appearance in Mr. Pastor's Theatre in seven years............HARRY MONTAGUE
CLARENCE EVERMONT, Arthur's chum at college......JACQUES KRUGER
Karl, a German friend of Arthur's..................Bonnie Runnells
Ebenezer, a high-toned waiter in the Haviland Mansion..........Frank White
Michael Olliver, a rich widower, a particular friend of the Haviland's...Frank Girard
Walter Haviland, Arthur's father, a wealthy retired merchant..H. S. Woodhull
Fred, a friend and visitor of Arthur's..................F. H. Clarke
Caroline, Arthur's sweet cousin, a real nice girl.............Carrie Duncan
Martha, Olliver's only daughter, pretty and accomplished......Sophie Duncan
Mrs. Miranda Haviland, formerly a society belle, but now Arthur's fond and loving stepmother, who doesn't object, however, to him calling her "Ma;" "but then it does seem so funny you know".Jennie Satterlee
Kitty, waiting maid, also at Haviland's...........................Florence Bell
Violet......... (Young friends of Arthur's who have been) ....Lillian White
Emily......... { invited to spend a week or two at the } ......Nelly Hoyt
Clara...... (seashore at the Haviland mansion) ..Mabel Runnells

PLOT.

The action of the comedy transpires in the house and grounds of the elegant Haviland Villa at Long Branch, in midsummer, and it being the occasion of Arthur Haviland's birthday, his parents and friends who are visiting them agree to give Arthur a Fancy Dress Garden Party, incidental to which there will be introduced bright, sparkling, popular music, gems from Comic Opera, catchy songs and choruses, a whirlwind of pure fun and pleasant surprises, terminating with the last figure of the enchanting Terpsichorean fantasie

THE DUDE LANCIERS.

in which the ladies will appear as DUDINES and wear magnificent new costumes, and the gentlemen will introduce some of the latest Fashion Follies of the NEW YORK DUDE.

The debonair performer Harry Montague, who wrote and starred in *The Dudes at Long Branch*, in a cabinet photo by Napoleon Sarony, c. 1870s.

But it seems that Olive's 1868 version of the same script with different names set at Narragansett Bay and called simply *Surf!* had made a big splash with Boston audiences first! Logan knew how to get as much mileage as possible out of her writings. New Yorkers also enjoyed Harry Montague's production of *The Dudes at Long Branch*, a musical comedy presented at Tony Pastor's theater in the 1870s. It was not known to be written for other resorts!

On Broadway

The first public theater at Long Branch , the Long Branch Opera House, was built in the 1880s on the west side of Washington Street, near Broadway. It was a venue for professional troupes from New York but in later years was used for amateur productions. Perhaps the most popular playhouse of all, however, was the Theatre Comique, an enclosed beer garden located at the back of the Sans Souci Hotel. Next, the Broadway Theater was built on Broadway across from the Steinbach's store and, until 1904; it was on the B.F. Keith vaudeville circuit.

The Broadway at Long Branch presented previews (tryouts) of shows before they opened on New York's "Great White Way" throughout the 1910s and 1920s. Programs show that it became "Reade's Broadway" in the 1920s. In 1931, it was remodeled and reopened as The Paramount, a movie palace operated by the Paramount Publix chain belonging to Walter Reade. The Strand located right across from the Paramount was a movie house built in 1915 by Reade that closed in the early 1970s when the Walter Reade movie theater chain went bankrupt.

Reade's Broadway Theatre
LONG BRANCH

Edgar Selwyn Presents the Hilarious Comedy

"Gentlemen Prefer Blondes"

By Anita Loos and John Emerson
An adaptation of Anita Loos' book of the same name.
Staged by Edgar Selwyn

Cast in the order of their appearance

Dorothy Shaw	Edna Hibbard
Harry, a steward	Harold Thomas
Gloria Atwell	Ruth Raymonde
Lorelei Lee	June Walker
Henry Spoffard	Frank Morgan
Lady Beekman	Grace Hampton
Sir Francis Beekman	Percy Ames
Mrs. Spoffard	Mrs. Jacques Martin
Miss Chapman	Katharine Brook
Leon, a hall boy	Daniel Wolf
Connie	Vivian Purcell
Robert Broussard	Georges Romain
Louis Broussard	Adrian Rosley
Gus Eisman	Arthur S. Ross
H. Gilbertson Montrose	Bruce Huntley
Dickie	Edwina Prie
Willie Gwynn	Roy Gorham
Lulu	Grace Burgess
Herb	Richard Brandlon
Ann Spoffard	Grace Cornell
Old Spoffard	Will T. Hays

Synopsis of Scenes

ACT I—Royal Suite on an ocean liner.
ACT II—A sitting room in the Ritz Hotel, Paris.
ACT III—Lorelei's apartment, New York

Miss Loos and Mr. Emerson wish to acknowledge their indebtedness to Mr. Selwyn for many excellent suggestions made during rehearsals of the play.   Gowns and hats by Frances, Ltd.

Scenes designed by Raymond Sovey and painted by Bergman Studios.

The "Grey's" Cigarettes used in this production being furnished by Benson & Hedges, 435 Fifth Avenue, New York

Shoes for this production from Saks, New York. Hosiery used in this production supplied by Van Raalte.

Canada Dry Ginger Ale used in this production.

For Mr. Selwyn

General Manager	John M. Zwicki
Business Manager	James H. Palser
General Stage Manager	William Postance
Press Representative	Marian Spitzer
Stage Manager	Adrian Rosley

ALL NEXT WEEK
HAROLD LLOYD
In His Latest and Best Comedy
"FOR HEAVEN SAKE"

A program representative of the numerous 1920s Broadway bound shows that were tried out at Long Branch before they opened in New York. In 1926, Anita Loos' stage adaptation of her novel *Gentlemen Prefer Blondes* featuring June Walker proved to be a hit. It was revised in 1949 as a Broadway musical starring the fabulous Carol Channing as Lorelei Lee. In 1953 the show was made into the now classic movie musical with Marilyn Monroe as Lorelei. *Moss Archives.*

READE'S

BROADWAY THEATRE

FRIDAY AND SATURDAY, SEPT. 23-24
Matinee Saturday, Sept. 24

Anton F. Scibilia Presents

Mae West in
"THE WICKED AGE"

A Comedy Drama in Three Acts
By Mae West

Staged by Edward Elsner

Characters in the order of their appearance

Aunt Elizabeth	Emily Francis
Ruth Carson	Doris Haslett
Willie Weller	Hassell Brooks
Gloria Scott	Ruth Hunter
Robert Carson	Hal Clarendon
Mr. Hathaway	Carroll Daly
John Ferguson	Francis Reynolds
Frenchy, the Count	Charles La Torre
Mrs. Robert Carson	Mathilde Baring
Evelyn 'Babe' Carson	MAE WEST
Bob Miles	Harry W. Williams
Al. Smalley	Hub White
Tom Grange	William Laggan
Jack Stratford	Raymond Jarno
George Smith	Harold Leonard
Lou Ginsberg	Harry W. Carter
Gladys Drake	Louise Kirtland
Neil Browne	Ethel Maynard
Polly Ackerman	Gene Woods
Annie Lawrence	Billy Le Seur
Harry Dempster	David Newell
Mack Hadden	Hal Findlay
Bert Astor	Arthur Boran
Stephany Joy	Veritza Winters
Norma Faire	Wilva Davis
Elinor Dane	Mildred Cornell
Mrs. Dane	Anita Lewis
Mrs. Joy	Mary Moore
Dan	Robert J. Rice
Joe	Gene Williams
Maggie McShane	Peggy Doran
Kepper Slattery	Louis Mountjoy
Sergeant MacDonald	A. Miller
Marty Jones	Harold Mayes
Sam Williams	Thomas Waller
Henry Lee	Thomas Morris
Nanine	Georgie Clarke
Dick Adams	Ed. Norman
Henry Arthur	Edwin Edwards
House Detective	A. Miller
Dr. Andrews	Carroll Daly

Bathing Girls, Visitors, Venders.

ACT I.—Home of Robert Carson, Bridgetown, N. J.   Time—evening.

ACT II.—Episode 1.—Moonlight Park.   An afternoon two weeks later.   Episode 2.—The same.   Midnight.

Between the first and second episodes, curtain will be lowered for one minute to denote the lapse of time.

ACT III.—Babe Carson's apartment, New York. One month later.

Negligees worn by Miss West created by Mr. Sam Mayo.   Executed by Mayo Undergarment Company, New York.

Slickers worn in second act furnished by Duro-Gloss Raincoat Company.

Toujours Moi perfume furnished by Corday, 15 Rue de La Paix, Paris.

Shoes worn by Miss West created by Cammeyer, New York.

In 1927, *The Wicked Age*, with the controversial Mae West previewed at Long Branch. It only lasted for nineteen performances on Broadway (New York). A reviewer called the play, an expose of bathing beauty contests, "tame" after West's previous show that was titled *Sex*. The following year she had great success with *Diamond Lil*. Mae West, who wrote most of her plays, also starred in movies, staying vivacious and performing until her death in 1980 at the age of eighty seven. *Moss Archives.*

A vintage postcard of the sensual star Mae West who created a stir with New Jersey Shore tryout theater audiences in the 1920s and 1930s.

A 1939 postcard looking west on Broadway, Long Branch, of The Paramount (reconstructed from the old Broadway Theatre and reopened in 1931) on the left and The Strand on the right, both movie houses belonging to the Walter Reade organization. The Strand no longer exists, and the Paramount (without the tower) has been a paint store since the early 1960s, but may be renovated as an arts center.

Outdoor Delights

Besides theaters and indoor entertainments, there were traveling circuses, carnivals, and wild west shows. They came to town, set up their tents, and stayed a few days, and brought fun and thrills to young and old alike.

Ocean Park was located by the boardwalk at Broadway and Ocean Avenue. It provided a great space for outdoor concerts in the early years of the twentieth century as evidenced in this vintage postcard.

The Carlisle Indian School Band, a star attraction, stands on the steps of the Long Branch Casino annex for this 1906 real photo postcard. The school (1879-1918) in Carlisle, Pennsylvania, was the first federally funded school for Native Americans to be established off a reservation. Their football team gained fame in the early twentieth century and the great American athlete Jim Thorpe participated in sports there.

"Society circuses" in which local people performed to raise money for charities were prevalent in the late nineteenth and early twentieth centuries. Whenever they could find the time, professional performers who summered or lived in the shore area did their best to participate in benefit performances, just as many stars do today. Children's carnivals and baby parades, horse shows and dog shows – all these promotional events and more were part of the entertainment scene at the Monmouth County shore. Blackface minstrel shows, considered offensive today, were also popular entertainment during this period. Various groups and organizations often put on minstrel shows until the mid-twentieth century.

America's great early clown, Dan Rice, pictured here in a mid-nineteenth century image, whose ancestry is linked with the Long Branch area, was born in New York City in 1823. The benevolent jester, credited with expressions used today such as "jump on the bandwagon" and "one horse show," wore many hats. Besides training his learned pig named Lord Byron, Rice was a political satirist, dancer, writer, a model for the character of Uncle Sam, and a candidate for President of the United States in 1868! He made a fortune in show business and donated much to charities but died penniless in 1900 while living with relatives at Long Branch. His grave remained unmarked until 1976 when Monmouth County descendants honored him with a "Dan Rice Day," an event that financed his grave marker at the Old First United Methodist Cemetery in West Long Branch. *Circus World Museum, Baraboo, Wisconsin.*

Another theatrical venue in the Long Branch area should be mentioned – the outdoor "floating" theater at Pleasure Bay Park, presumably part of Riverside Park built in 1898 on the South Shrewsbury River at Branchport Creek by the Patten Line steamboat company and the Atlantic Coast Railway. The inexpensive amusements at the end of the line attracted middle class visitors reflecting a change in the clientele coming to Long Branch.

Curtain Going Up

Hundreds of theatrical people visited or performed at Long Branch over the years. It would be impossible to tell all their stories and to merely list their names would not give the reader a proper look back at what the players were like or how they lived. Short biographies are presented here to describe some of the most influential of the performers, those who summered and those who stayed permanently.

And now…introducing the stars of Long Branch…

A c.1905 postcard of the open air theatre at Pleasure Bay Park that featured live productions such as Gilbert and Sullivan operettas. Various amusements and food concessions were available at the park near the steamboat dock for the increasing numbers of day trippers visiting Long Branch.

Prince of Players - Edwin Booth

"He was greatly attached to his horses, and skillful in the management of them. He had several narrow escapes while driving, one of which I witnessed as a child. It occurred at Long Branch, behind his favorite horse Nellie, when his buggy was overturned and he was thrown beneath his horse's feet. With remarkable agility and presence of mind, he picked himself up, quieted his horse and then, hastening to me, tenderly soothed my alarm, and jokingly remarked that his spotless suit of white flannels was hopelessly ruined." From *Recollections by His Daughter and Letters to her and to his Friends* by Edwina Grossman Booth.

Perhaps the most talked about star to summer at Long Branch was the great American tragedian, Edwin Booth. From 1867-1871, he enjoyed the pastoral haven of Elberon (a section of Long Branch) where he could spend time with his daughter, Edwina. Her mother, Booth's first wife actress Mary Devlin, died in 1863 when Edwina was only a toddler. At Long Branch, Edwin Booth did not partake in the flashy activities at the plush oceanfront hotels and gambling clubs. He preferred being surrounded by close theatrical friends in the quieter environs of the actor's colony where he would often go for drives in the country.

From the late 1860s till the early years of the 20th century, cabinet photos (4 ½" x 6 ½") by well-known photographers were sold as souvenirs to admiring fans. In this one taken by Napoleon Sarony, Edwin Booth is seen as the infamous Iago from Shakespeare's Othello. Although thousands of prints were originally made of the souvenir photos, the small numbers that survive today are very collectible.

EDWIN BOOTH .
37 UNION SQR. N. Y.

The Shadows of Lincoln's Assassin

The soulful eyes of Edwin Booth seem to gaze out wistfully from his portraits, forever reminding the world of his sorrow. Emerging from the dark shadows created by his brother John Wilkes' dastardly act, Edwin had managed to regain his reputation, successfully continue his career and take care of his daughter. Edwina's account of her father's good humor after a driving accident, illustrates a seldom-heard side of Edwin's personality.

The debonair actor John Wilkes Booth assassinated President Lincoln on April 14, 1865, at Ford's Theater in Washington D.C. not long after the Confederate surrender to the Union Army at Appomattox. John Wilkes, a pro-Confederate extremist, snuck into the box where Mr. and Mrs. Lincoln were enjoying a performance of *Our American Cousin*, shot the President point blank, and then leaped onto the stage. He escaped to Virginia despite a broken leg, but after an extensive manhunt was cornered by federal soldiers on April 26 and killed.

Edwin Booth, exhausted and shattered by his brother's fanatical act, withdrew from the theater and public life until the following year. Edwin had nothing to do with the assassination but, of course, his name was linked with that of his brother who would always be remembered for killing President Abraham Lincoln. Edwin, even today, is often identified first as "John Wilkes Booth's brother" and then as one of America's most distinguished actors. Besides the association with John Wilkes, Edwin had to overcome other difficulties throughout his lifetime as well. His troubles began in childhood as he grew up with a father who today would be considered abusive and alcoholic. Edwin was the son of English-born actor Junius Brutus Booth (1796-1852). Edwin's father deserted his wife and wed Mary Ann Holmes, and they immigrated to America. The couple settled on a farm near Belair Maryland and had a total of ten children but some of them did not survive childhood. Three of their sons became actors. Junius Brutus Booth Jr. (b.1821), Edwin (b.1833) and John Wilkes (b.1838). The youngest child, Joseph, tried acting for only a very brief time, didn't have what it takes and then studied medicine instead.

Off to California

At the age of thirteen, Edwin began to accompany his eccentric father on theatrical tours as his companion and he tried to keep his Dad sober. In 1849, Edwin made his acting debut at the Boston Museum performing a small part in a production of *Richard III* that starred his father. He took over the role of Richard III when his Booth Sr. was unable to go on stage.

Edwin traveled to California with his father in 1852 where they acted in plays under the management of older brother Junius Brutus Booth Jr. On his way back to Maryland alone, their father, Junius Sr. died.

Edwin's True Love

In 1860, Edwin Booth married the pretty actress Mary Devlin, who is often said to be Edwin's one and only true love. The actor suffered a catastrophic loss when his young wife died from illness in 1863 and he was left with their small daughter, Edwina, to care for. Edwin, with traits perhaps inherited from his father, was known to drink excessively and was not at Mary's side when she died, reportedly because he was too disorientated from the effects of alcohol.

This carte de visite photo by J. Gurney & Sons, New York, is of tragedian Edwin Booth in the early 1860s. The small carte de visites (4 ¼" x 2 ½") that reached their height of popularity around the Civil War era are valued photographic collectibles today, especially those of military and political figures and of theatrical stars.

The Brothers in *Julius Caesar*

In 1864, the three Booth brothers who were actors starred in a one-night benefit performance of Shakespeare's *Julius Caesar* at New York's Winter Garden Theatre of which Edwin was a co-manager. The performance, to raise money for a statue of Shakespeare to be placed in Central Park, was the one and only time the three would appear together in a play. Edwin played Brutus, Junius Brutus Jr. was Cassius and John Wilkes portrayed Marc Antony. Interestingly, their one performance together was in a play about a political assassination. Beginning the next day, Edwin portrayed Hamlet and would do so consecutively for one hundred performances.

Conspiracy Hatched at Long Branch?

Not long after the closing of *Hamlet*, a great success for Edwin, the appalling news from Washington that President Lincoln had been shot rocked the nation. Volumes have been written about the assassination over the years and interest in the tragedy and numerous theories about the event continue to arise.

A few stories even surfaced suggesting that John Wilkes, while staying at The United States Hotel in Long Branch in 1863, plotted to kidnap President Lincoln. There is no tangible evidence to support this story but rumor has it that Copperheads went to see John at his hotel room and their visits appeared secretive and aroused suspicions. John Wilkes no doubt visited Long Branch at that time, but it is pure speculation to think that he devised such a scheme there.

The Best Theater Yet

The distraught Edwin had gone into isolation after his brother's crime but returned to the stage in 1866. The following year, a horrible fire destroyed the Winter Garden Theatre and Booth ambitiously decided to build his own theater. Construction soon began on The Booth Theatre, located at the southeast corner of 23rd Street and Sixth Avenue. The state-of-the-art building, designed by the architectural firm of Renwick and Sands, had the best possible fire protection installed and cost a million dollars, a vast amount at that time.

Edwin Booth's magnificent new playhouse opened on February 3, 1869, with a performance of *Romeo and Juliet*. During that same year, Booth was to spend a good amount of time at Long Branch whenever he could get a chance for some much needed rest. He was courting his lovely young leading lady Mary McVicker, who played Juliet to his Romeo, and Mary's family had a house in the Elberon section of Long Branch. Mary's stepfather James McVicker owned the cottage that was built for him by Elberon founder L.B. Brown. The house called "Meerschaum Villa" (located near the intersection of the Deal Turnpike, now Norwood Ave., and Wooley Ave., now Park Ave.) was purchased by actress Maggie Mitchell in 1875 (see next chapter). Edwin Booth first met Mary McVicker in Chicago while he was appearing there. Mary's stepfather was James McVicker a well-known actor and theater manager in Chicago. McVicker was fond of his step daughter and always looking out for her best interests.

The Booth Theatre at the southeast corner of West 23rd St. and Sixth Avenue, opened on February, 3, 1869. Situated in what was the heart of New York's theater district at that time, the theater that Edwin Booth built featured an elaborate stage, scenic workshops, and state of the art systems in case of fire.

Here Comes the Bride

About four months after the opening of the new theater, Edwin Booth and Mary Runnion McVicker were married at the McVicker cottage in Elberon, on June 7, 1869, and Mary's grandfather, the Reverend Myers, came all the way from California to officiate. Not much is known about the wedding, that was said to be attended only by a few friends including actor Edwin Adams and his wife who had a cottage called "Seaview" nearby.

Edwin told a friend at the end of the summer: "My little wife is a quaint, cosy (sic), loveable little body, and we get on famously. She and Edwina are all in all."[1] It was Mary's first marriage. Booth's main motivation for this second marriage seemed to be for Edwina to have a mother once again, rather than for him to have a new wife.

A Difficult Birth Leads to Madness

Mary became pregnant a few months after their marriage, and she had already stopped acting. Mary and Edwin took up residence in rooms above the Booth Theatre. Her pregnancy dragged on for a month beyond the due date. It was an unbearably hot Fourth of July in 1870, when Mary finally went into labor. At their residence over the theater, the small-framed Mary's agonizing labor continued until a doctor delivered the child using instruments. Sadly, the baby's head was severely damaged and the ten pound boy named "Edgar" died within a few hours after birth. His mother recovered physically from the terrible ordeal, but her sorrow was overwhelming and emotionally she would never be the same. She was said to suffer from "nervous instability." Her behavior became erratic and some people said she simply went mad.

He Built His House of Bricks

The Jersey Shore seemed like a fine place for Mary to recuperate after the trauma of losing the baby. Her parents still owned Meerschaum Villa, but Booth had a cottage of his own erected nearby, perhaps wanting to have a little privacy from his in laws. He had made an offer for $ 40,000 to buy the McVicker place, but his father-in-law advised him to think it over, as he felt that Edwin was trying to satisfy poor Mary's "every whim."

J.H. McVicker's Elberon cottage "Meershaum Villa," was the site of Edwin Booth's marriage to Mary McVicker in 1869. Booth (who is hard to see by the doorway) happened to be visiting when G.W. Pach took this photo in 1868 for *Schenck's Album of Long Branch.* Booth's little daughter Edwina is in the porch hammock. *Moss Archives.*

The magnificent home that was completed in 1871, on the southwest corner of Park Ave. (then called Wooley Ave.) and Larchwood Avenues, was only a short distance from McVicker's place. Edwin, Mary, and Edwina lived in their splendid new red brick house with a high tower called "Fairlawns" during the summer of 1871, but by the end of the year the place had to be sold due to Booth's increasing financial difficulties.

Economic Woes

In October of 1871, Booth purchased his financial partner Robertson's holdings in the theater, $ 240,000, that was paid as $ 100,000 in money and real estate. The real estate was "Mary's Long Branch place." The property was legally in Mary's name.[2] Poor financial management of Booth's theater brought about its decline while Edwin's younger brother, Joseph Booth, was acting as the treasurer. And so, the marvelous "Fairlawns" that Booth built, his house of bricks with the high tower, would have to be sold within a year after the family moved in. The ideal world that Booth had tried to build for his little family was crumbling. Now there was one more reason for the great tragedian to look so doleful.

Collection Col. T. A. Brown
Edwin Booth and his second wife (Mary McVicker) and daughter, Edwina Booth Grossman

Edwin Booth, his second wife Mary McVicker, and his daughter by his first marriage, Edwina, pose for a formal portrait in the mid 1870s. *The Theatre*, May 1904.

A stereograph from 1871 taken by Pach Brothers shows "Booth's Cottage," an imposing brick mansion with a tower that was located at the intersection of what is now Park and Larchwood Avenues in Ocean Township. The house was in existence until the 1940s. Stereographs were popular souvenir items purchased to be used with viewers called stereoscopes for parlor amusement.

Booth's Best Buddy

During his time at Elberon, Booth often saw his friend Lawrence Barrett, an actor who came from a struggling Irish immigrant family (his real name is believed to be "Brannigan"). Barrett was born in Paterson, New Jersey, in 1838, but raised in Detroit where he made his acting debut.

Edwin Booth's friend and business associate, the New Jersey born actor Lawrence Barrett is costumed for the role of Lanciotto in Boker's *Francesca da Rimini* in this 1870s cabinet photo by Napoleon Sarony. Barrett summered near Booth at Elberon.

He idolized Edwin Booth and became a great tragedian in his own right although he is not generally well known today. Eventually, Barrett became Booth's business partner and was somewhat of a theatrical historian. He wrote several books before his death in 1891.

Beware the Coming of the Railroad

On September 9, 1871, Edwin Booth wrote a letter to Lawrence Barrett in which he expressed his growing concern regarding the inevitable coming of the railroad near his sprawling Elberon property, "Fairlawns." Booth wrote to Barrett: "I have some (not very good) news for you. For several summers past an association of Methodists has been trying to establish a little one-horse village up the road toward Shark River and have used every endeavor to have a railroad running from Long Branch to their camp grounds at Ocean Grove."[3] Booth warns Barrett that the proposed route appears to run right though Barrett's lot close to his "little white house and grove of trees." He confides that "Coming so close to me destroys all my interest in the place…"[4]

Apparently, Barrett had some land with a "little white house" and was planning to build a larger home near Booth's Elberon cottage. It is not certain if Barrett owned the property. One possibility is that Booth or someone else was renting land to Barrett.

The Dilemma of Development

No doubt Booth was worried that his bucolic summer retreat would be threatened by the coming of the railroad. (The railroad did indeed come through the area in 1875, opening up the Monmouth County Shore to more visitors.) Interestingly, some of Booth's comments about land conservation and over development reflect the concerns of many people today that were clearly being foreshadowed well over a century ago. Booth's letter may, though his concerns about his real estate were sincere, have also been masking his financial problems with the theater. If he could not afford his New Jersey Shore home anymore, he could simply say he was selling due to dissatisfaction with the encroaching railroad.

Old Oaks - The Clark Estate

In 1875, "Fairlawns" was sold to the publisher of the *Newark Daily Advertiser*, T.T. Kinney. The estate later changed hands, but stayed in the Kinney family, when one of Kinney's daughters married William Campbell Clark of the Clark Thread Company. The estate, which the Clark family owned until the 1940s, was then known as "Old Oaks" and that is supposedly how the area got the name "Oakhurst."

A c.1905 postcard produced by New York publisher Arthur Livingston provides a fine view of the former Edwin Booth estate "Fairlawns" long after it became "Old Oaks," the home of the head of the Clark Thread Company and his family.

The Booth Family

On November 13, 1881, Mary McVicker Booth died, weakened by her mental health problems. Edwin continued his acting career and his friend Barrett became his closest and most trusted business associate.

Although Edwin did not own a place at Long Branch after 1871, he would visit Long Branch to see his mother, brother Joseph, and sister Rosalie, who lived on the splendid oceanfront. In the 1870s, the youngest of Junius Brutus Booth's children, "Joe," had purchased an oceanfront cottage at Long Branch that was adjacent to the Atlantic Hotel. Their mother, Mary Holmes Booth, stayed there as well as their sister Rosalie, who was devoted to caring for her mother. Rosalie was known as the reticent Booth.

Joe Booth was the treasurer of Edwin Booth's theater and apparently did not have the proper business acumen, as he did a poor job. He worked as a physician, although requirements for the profession were quite different in those days, and he did not receive a full-fledged medical degree until 1894. That same year, he married and continued to own the Long Branch house.

Down by the Boardwalk

The Joseph Booth waterfront house was located on Ocean Avenue and is identified on an *1885 Tourist's Map of Long Branch* just one house to the south of the Atlantic Hotel on the corner of Railroad Avenue (today this is Pavilion Ave).[5] Next to the Booth house two homes owned by Mr. Bispham are indicated. A deed shows that Joseph A. Booth purchased the land in 1873 from Charles Bispham and Samuel Morris.[6]

There were many changes along the popular oceanfront during the late nineteenth century but during the entire period that Joseph Booth maintained his home there, it was a lively scene. One can imagine what life there was like for Booth's mother and his sister, Rosalie. Most likely, they enjoyed watching the daily parade of fashions on the boardwalk, taking drives in a stylish horse and carriage, and simply breathing in the healthy sea air, so refreshing compared to the mugginess at their New York City residence. There is an "almost certainly incorrect story" that someone beat up the docile Rosalie at Joseph's house (Long Branch) because she was John Wilkes' sister.[7]

Booth's mother, Mary Ann Holmes Booth, died in 1885. She really never got over the shock of her beloved son John shooting the President. The dying assassin's last words are often quoted as: "Tell Mother I died for my country. I did what I thought was best." Rosalie died in 1889, reportedly at Joe's Long Branch house.

The Final Years - Gramercy Park

In 1888, Booth founded The Players, an association for theatrical and other notable men at Gramercy Park, New York, where he lived in an upstairs apartment. Booth's last appearance was on April 4, 1891, as Hamlet at the Brooklyn Academy of Music. His friend Barrett died in 1891.

On June 7, 1893, Edwin Booth died in his New York bedroom at The Players. A statue of the actor was placed in the center of the square at Gramercy Park, across from his home in 1918 as an enduring tribute to his greatness.

The Players is still in existence as an updated and active club and houses the Hampden-Booth Theatre Library.

A Lonely Figure by the Sea

The July 1905 issue of a popular magazine, *The Delineator*, published a romanticized version of Edwin's time at Long Branch. The article, called "Romances of Summer Resorts," included a description of Edwin Booth on the Long Branch boardwalk:

> "When the world of Long Branch was enjoying its dinner a lonely figure often stood on the boardwalk and gazed at the ocean covered with the glory of sunset. The man seemed to be holding communion with the waves. Like a shade fresh from Stygian regions his form was silhouetted against the golden glow. Softly the night winds would creep up from the ocean and blow apart his black coat. He would turn and the chance pedestrian would come face to face with Edwin Thomas Booth."[8]

The Merry Cricket – Maggie Mitchell

With a toss of her golden curls and a swish of her apron, Maggie Mitchell captivated nineteenth century American audiences as the title character in *Fanchon the Cricket*. From the 1860s to the 1890s, the catchy name "Cricket" became "inseparably linked" with Maggie.

Ageless Beauty

The petite performer never seemed to age. It was amazing how she could play the same role as Fanchon successfully for over thirty years during an era when most people seemed to look far older than they were (at least by today's standards they did). The sprightly Maggie appeared in a variety of dramatic roles; however, it is for her portrayal of the merry Cricket that she is best remembered.

Maggie Mitchell starred in the title role of *Fanchon the Cricket* for decades. This charming stereo of "the Cricket" by New York photographers J. Gurney & Son dates to the 1860s. Maggie's pose was probably considered quite alluring in its day!

Early Life

Born Margaret Julia Mitchell, in New York City in 1837 (some sources list her birth year as 1832), Maggie's father, Charles Mitchell, a theatrical manager, and her mother, Anna Dodson Mitchell, came to America from England. Maggie was said to have been on the stage from the time she learned to walk. This was probably an exaggeration, and her true debut was at the age of fourteen in *The Soldier's Daughter.* The elfin Maggie then played several boys parts including the title role in *Oliver Twist* and Edward the young Prince of Wales in Shakespeare's *Richard III.*

Three Sisters

Maggie's half sisters were also stage stars. Her sister Emma Mitchell, who started in 1853 as a *danseuse* in New York, began her career as an actress in 1858. Emma was never as well known as Maggie or their sister Mary Lomax Mitchell (their mother was previously married to an actor named Joseph Lomax) who became popular with the American public. Born in 1831, Mary made her first stage appearance in 1855 at Newark, New Jersey, playing the part of Topsey in a production of *Uncle Tom's Cabin.* Mary was even billed on a theatre poster as the "first woman song and dance artist in America."[1]

The Chic Cricket

It was Maggie who dazzled theatergoers and ranks as the most successful member of her talented family. In the early days of her career, there was a "Maggie Mitchell craze" in Cleveland where "young men took to wearing Maggie Mitchell scarves, hats, and the like."[2] The petite dynamo became a trendsetter and always wore the latest fashions. In photographs of her in street clothes, she shows off flattering hats, stylish dresses, and exquisite jewelry including dangling earrings. Although common hairstyles of her day featured pristine chignons and smooth styles, she often let her curly tresses hang loose and flowing. Some of the important plays (several of them written especially for her) that Maggie starred in during the course of her long career were *Jane Eyre*, *Little Barefoot*, *Ray*, *Mignon*, *The Pearl of Savoy*, and *The Lady of Lyons*.

SARONY,   680 BROADWAY.

MAGGIE MITCHELL.

Trendsetter Maggie Mitchell looks fashionable yet relaxed in this portrait, c.1880 by Napoleon Sarony, the great portrait photographer so well known for his theatrical pictures. The belle of the Long Branch actors' colony, Maggie often wore modish jewelry like the large dangling earrings seen here.

Shadow Dancing

Maggie excelled in all of the roles she played, but it was for her characterization of *Fanchon* that she became the darling of the American public. There were several dramatizations based upon the story *La Petite Fadette* by French author George Sand, one of the most significant female writers of the nineteenth century. Maggie Mitchell produced an adaptation of Sand's story in which she portrayed Fanchon, a mysterious young country girl whose mother had deserted her. Her grandmother, Old Fadet, whom villagers believed to be a witch, raised the child. Fanchon is described as "piquant" and "sharp-tongued." On June 3, 1861, Maggie's older half sister Mary (who was then Mrs. Albaugh) played the part of Old Fadet.

A Favorite of Abe Lincoln

Maggie premiered her version of *Fanchon the Cricket* in 1861 at the St. Charles Theatre in New Orleans. As the story goes, her mother leased Laura Keene's Theatre in New York and Maggie opened in *Fanchon* there on June 9, 1862. Although she appeared in the South during the war, Maggie was known to be a staunch supporter of the North. When the Civil War ended, she was playing in Mobile, Alabama, and declared that she was "the first woman to raise the 'Stars and Stripes' in Mobile!"[3]

MAGGIE MITCHELL. ("Shadow Dance.")

Cabinet Series

Maggie Mitchell observes her mysterious silhouette as she performs her original "Shadow Dance." The moonlit scene provided a great piece of theatrical magic described as "weird and elfish" that enhanced productions of *Fanchon the Cricket*. A "Newsboy" 1890s cabinet photo reprint of an earlier photograph, offered as a tobacco premium.

Fanchon the Cricket proved to be a favorite among American theatergoers and President Abraham Lincoln was one of Maggie's fans. Legend has it that she also appealed to Lincoln's assassin, actor John Wilkes Booth. Photographs of several actresses were allegedly found on John Wilkes Booth's body when he was killed, including one of Maggie. Today, she is sometimes said to have been romantically involved with John Wilkes Booth, but this is almost certainly a myth that has been exaggerated over the years.[4] She was his contemporary, they most likely knew each other from theater engagements, but that appears to have been the extent of the relationship.

The Cricket's Business Acumen

Most everyone knew that Maggie, the adored Cricket was a great actress, but the public may not have been aware that she also was a talented entrepreneur. The merry little Cricket became the influential queen bee of the summer actor's colony at Long Branch. She is described as being "intense, "hardworking" and even "severe."

Around the end of the Civil War, Maggie with her manager-husband Harry T. Paddock, and their children, Fanchon (after the character of course!) and Harry, lived in a cottage on the south side of Cedar Avenue. The lot where their home was located, now part of Monmouth University, West Long Branch, was apparently one of several lots that belonged to the actress. A number of choice properties listed as belonging to "M.J. Paddock" are marked on atlases of Long Branch from the 1870s.

A Long Engagement

Maggie Mitchell and Harry Paddock of Cleveland had courted each other for almost fourteen years before they married on October 15, 1868. The following summer, in 1869, Maggie was gravely ill and "in danger for some time" but pulled through the crisis. During her illness, Maggie's mother died in New York, so it was an especially difficult time for her.[5]

The couple divorced in 1888 after twenty years of marriage. By the following year, Maggie married Charles Abbott, her leading man who became her theatrical manager. Maggie was fifty-one years old when she married Abbott. What most certainly would be "over the hill" for most women in Maggie's day did not seem to apply to the ageless Cricket.

Victorian males ruled at work and at home, but in the theater women were able to be managers and even work on a fairly equal basis with men. Maggie eventually ran her own theater company. Aspiring writers who would mail their scripts to her were disappointed to receive rejections. Most of them were merely trying to copy Fanchon.

An astute investor, Maggie put money into real estate and bought several parcels of land at Long Branch. The rural New Jersey shore began to develop rapidly after the Civil War and lots were going quickly. Although she wanted to summer in the area where she and her family could have some peace and quiet, she must have also recognized the growth potential of the area. She maintained residences in both New York City where she also bought properties and at Long Branch for most of her life.

Good Times at Cricket Lodge

In 1875, Maggie purchased James McVicker's Elberon cottage, "Meerschaum Villa" near the southwest corner of Park and Norwood Avenues (now Ocean Township). (The home was the site of the 1869 marriage ceremony of McVicker's stepdaughter Mary and actor Edwin Booth). After Maggie acquired Meerschaum Villa in 1875, it soon became known as "Cricket Lodge" and there she entertained many of her theatrical friends for more than forty years. Rustic and quiet, set back about two miles from the bustling Long Branch oceanfront, her place was a country retreat where Maggie enjoyed the soothing atmosphere away from the footlights, away from the noise of New York City.

A c.1870 stereograph by photographer G.W. Pach of "Miss Maggie Mitchell's Cottage" provides a rare glimpse into the private life of the star at Long Branch. The woman sitting in a chair is most likely Maggie. This is apparently the house where she lived on Cedar Ave. just before she purchased McVicker's "Meershaum Villa" (Norwood Ave.) in 1875, the home that was would be affectionately known as "Cricket Lodge."

Olive's Vivid Imagery

A description of Cricket Lodge was published in an article about Long Branch by well known actress and author Olive Logan. The feature appeared in the September 1876 issue of *Harpers New Monthly Magazine*. Olive Logan's style exemplifies the flowery writing that was commonplace:

"The cottages occupied by the dramatic fraternity present no features differing from others unless it be a superiority in the matter of interior adornment. Their luxury in this respect is, indeed, in several cases very striking, the reason being partly, perhaps that the players have no town homes as a rule, their winters being mostly passed in traveling, and dwelling (in) hotels."

"So their summer homes, to which they hie for rest and as soon as their 'season' of active labor is over, become in a peculiar sense dear to them. One of the most conspicuous examples of the luxury of these homes is furnished in the cottage owned and occupied by Maggie Mitchell, 'The Cricket.' She owns a number of cottages and farms at Long Branch; the one in which she dwells was built by Edwin Booth and in its large parlor he was married."

Olive Logan was not completely correct. Edwin Booth was married there and then built a home just down the road, but did not build Meershaum Villa. Maggie purchased the home from Booth's father-in-law, James McVicker in 1875. Also, the engraving of Maggie's cottage accompanying Logan's article is believed to be of her earlier cottage on Cedar Ave., not Meerschaum Villa.

Domestic Spirit

The observations of Olive Logan in her *Harper's Weekly* article provide insight into the nature of the nineteenth century actor's colonies:

"All the evidences of an affectionate domestic spirit are abundant in this little artist's abode; and the same is true of the other homes of the Player Folk at Long Branch. Children make merry in their roomy halls; gray-haired parents sit at the hospitable board; the house-dog barks and the chickens cluck and the cattle low about these homes as about the homes of other good and gentle people.

Theatrical star and prolific author Olive Logan is the subject of this formal portrait from the 1870s. An early advocate of women's rights, she wrote books about the theater and descriptions of life at Long Branch where she was a frequent visitor. Wearing an elaborate dress and mantilla, she places her hands across her tummy for dramatic effect.

For the most part they are somewhat remote from the gay scene which looks to the sea, where pleasure holds her court in hotel parlors, on the lawns where the brass bands blare and up and down the drive."

Peace and Quiet

Olive Logan points out that the theatre people go to Long Branch for peace and quiet, not to be a part of the competitive and fashionable hotel life that existed simultaneously along the bluff and boardwalk. Few reports exist that describe the players mingling with the summer crowd at the hotels and gambling clubs although a number of them went to Monmouth Park racetrack. Accentuating the idyllic life of the celebrities, Logan writes:

> "The players rather favor a quieter mode of life in summer than that which is popular with the majority of visitors to Long Branch. They like to be near it, but they are seldom of it. Their time is passed in home hospitalities, in the entertainment of their friends, in reading the long summer hours away on their piazzas or lolling in tree-swung hammocks, and in driving bout the country in cozy family carriages, rather than in the feverish atmosphere of fashionable ball-rooms, the daily gambol in the surf, or the exciting delight of the gaming table."

The Cricket's Retirement

Cricket Lodge went through many changes as it was remodeled over the years. Maggie maintained a New York apartment but continued to spend much of her time at Long Branch after her withdrawal from acting in the mid 1890s. She seems to have slipped out of the limelight without any big "final" performance or notices of her retirement. Many companies still used the image of *Fanchon the Cricket* on their trade cards, advertisements, and premiums for many years.

The postmark on this postcard of Maggie Mitchell's Cricket Lodge at "Elberon-Long Branch" is from June 1907. The house has been totally remodeled since it was known as McVicker's "Meershaum Villa" in the late 1860s.

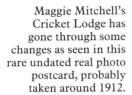

Maggie Mitchell's Cricket Lodge has gone through some changes as seen in this rare undated real photo postcard, probably taken around 1912.

After her retirement from the stage, Maggie Mitchell, or Mrs. Abbott as she was known, and her husband divided their time between Cricket Lodge and their elegant New York apartment. Abbott, formerly a well-known actor and manager, was "engaged in mercantile pursuits." "An accomplished young daughter resides with her, and a son is a rising young merchant in Boston. These are children by a former marriage."[6] Eventually, Fanchon married a man named Henry Mashey and the couple made their home in Long Branch.

It was hard for American audiences to lose their adored Cricket but times were changing and audacious ingénues were taking over:

Bas-relief images of Maggie Mitchell and other nineteenth century actresses appeared on pressed pattern glass. The actress motifs, modeled from popular stars' photographs, were made after the 1876 Philadelphia Centennial Exposition. They became popular household items in the 1880s and represented a growing respect for theatrical performers. They are popular collectibles today.

"Alas! the characters and the plays which served to make Maggie Mitchell so great a favorite with father and mothers, and so much beloved by every child, are no longer in fashion. Such things are too tame for the present day, since the rising generation of playgoers crave more highly seasoned food."[7]

The Passing of the Cricket

Obituaries vary as to the cause of Maggie's death on March 22, 1918. She was confined to her New York residence at 855 West End Ave. for the last months of her life from August 1917 until she passed away. Some reports say that she took a fall at Cricket Lodge in August that precipitated her death. Others simply say that she suffered "a breakdown."

Funeral services were held at the New York apartment. Many of her friends from the Long Branch area were present and her half-nephew actor Dodson Mitchell attended. Maggie was buried in the family plot at Brooklyn's Greenwood Cemetery.

Tiny cards that came as giveaways in packs of cigarettes often featured theatrical stars. A picture of Maggie Mitchell as Mignon is on this "Hall's Between the Acts" cigarette card from the late nineteenth century. Vintage tobacco items are popular collectibles today.

At the time when the leading lady of the Long Branch actor's colony died, moving pictures were gaining in popularity. Maggie never tried doing movies. Perhaps she would have, but they came too late in her career. When she died, silent films were being made in New Jersey. But, Hollywood was blooming, and many players were taking advantage of improvements in rail transportation and heading west. Stage folk from New York and Philadelphia still vacationed at the New Jersey Shore but the area was not the elite and peaceful haven that it was in the days when Maggie entertained friends and colleagues at Cricket Lodge.

No doubt the Cricket didn't want a lot of fanfare about her passing. She desired to go down in history as being vivacious and merry ... always chirping!

More Mitchells at Long Branch

Several theatrical members of Maggie's family also lived in the vicinity of the actor's colony at Long Branch. Maggie's older sister, Mary, married theatre producer James Albaugh (1837-1909) in July 1866 and they lived on the north side of Cedar Avenue, west of Norwood Avenue adjoining the property where the great actress Mary Anderson lived for a while. Mary Mitchell Albaugh died at Long Branch on June 22, 1908 and her husband James died at Long Branch in February of the following year.

A colorful lithograph of Maggie Mitchell as Fanchon on an 1894 advertising premium for McLaughlin's Coffee doesn't look much like her. Other celebrity pictures that consumers could send away for in the McLaughlin series included Queen Victoria, Abraham Lincoln, Prince Bismarck, and Mrs. Cleveland with Baby Ruth – quite an array of notables!

Broadway Bound – Julian Mitchell

Julian Mitchell, usually said to be a nephew of Maggie's (details of his birth and parentage are unclear) had a house on Norwood Avenue. Mitchell (1854-1926) began his theatrical career at Niblo's Garden, a famous downtown 19th century New York theater, and worked his way up to become one of the greatest Broadway musical directors of all time. His name appears on a program with his famous "Aunt Maggie" in plays such as *The Pearl of Savoy* when Julian played the part of "Pierrot" in 1880. Also, Maggie's other half nephew, Dodson Lomax, whom she raised after the death of his father became a well-known actor and used the name, Dodson L. Mitchell (1868 -1938).

Feeling the Beat

When Julian Mitchell began to lose his hearing, he turned to directing and found his true calling. He would rest his ear on the piano to feel the beat of the music in order to choreograph musicals.[8] Julian staged popular shows during the last decade of the nineteenth century including Charles Hoyt's hit play, *A Trip to Chinatown*. He developed a fast form of pacing and established a chorus line of glamorous women for Weber and Fields' productions.

From Oz to the Follies

In 1903, Julian directed *The Wizard of Oz*, the first stage adaptation of L. Frank Baum's tale. It was quite different from the version that most people think of today, the 1939 musical film classic with Judy Garland as Dorothy. In 1903, Mitchell also directed Victor Herbert's *Babes in Toyland*, another well-known show that had revivals on stage and screen. Legendary producer Florenz Ziegfeld recognized Julian Mitch-

Sheet music with songs from the *Ziegfeld Follies* was popular in the early twentieth century when most every home had a piano. This one is for "I'd Like to Put You in a Big Glass Case (and Look at You All Day)" a number from the 1924 revue staged by Julian Mitchell who lived in West Long Branch, NJ. The cover art is by illustrator Albert Vargas, the official illustrator for the Follies who became famous for his pin-up art of the 1940s.

ell's talent and hired him to direct the *Follies of 1907* (the first of the extravagant revues that would later be known as *The Ziegfeld Follies*) Mitchell went on to direct eight more Follies productions as well as many Broadway shows. A dancer in one of the productions told a story regarding the director's hearing loss. Once, while there was a storm with thunder booming outside, Julian Mitchell was rehearsing with his Follies dancers. Apparently, he heard the thunder faintly and asked the dancers, "Why are you girls shuffling your feet?"[9]

Teenage Bessie Clayton who married mature Follies director Julian Mitchell demonstrates her ability as a toe dancer in a classic pose. This is a Newsboy cabinet photo, c.1890s. "Newsboys," reprints of photos by famous theatrical photographers, were given away as premiums with tobacco purchases.

Enter Bessie Clayton

Julian Mitchell not only directed good-looking dancers, he married one of the greatest dancers Broadway has ever seen. He fell in love with a gorgeous young blonde who would become a star of the Follies; her name was Bessie Clayton.

Born in Philadelphia in 1883, Bessie got her start as a child dancer and was spotted by producer Charles Hoyt. She was brought to New York in 1896 by Hoyt and Thomas to appear in their popular production *A Trip to Chinatown.* But Bessie was under sixteen, the legal age for performers, and the Gerry Society tried to prevent her from going on stage. Also known as the New York Society for the Prevention of Cruelty to Children, the Gerry Society was founded in 1875 by lawyer and reformer Elbridge Thomas Gerry and Henry Bergh who started the SPCA. Although Bessie was so young she was said to be "well developed for one of her age." Supposedly, her parents were sent to a hiding place by the show's producers and the Gerry officers could not locate them for verification. Bessie would not admit her real age, and the show went on with Bessie delighting the New York audience.[10]

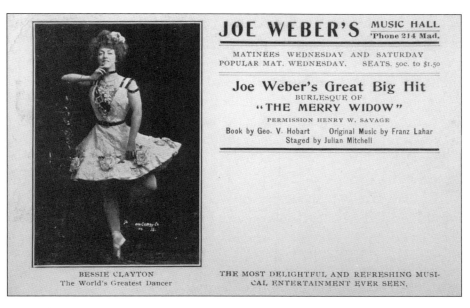

A c.1905 postcard advertising the hit show *The Merry Widow* features a photo of young Bessie Clayton, "The World's Greatest Dancer." The production was staged by her husband Julian Mitchell.

If Bessie Could Bounce!

Julian and Bessie married in 1899 when he was in his mid forties and she was still in her teens. An article from a theatrical publication pasted on a page in a vintage scrapbook c.1900 praises Bessie: "Such dancing was never known as Bessie Clayton's. Probably such dancing will never be seen again when Bessie is no more - which let it never be before 2000 A.D. There is a suspicion that Bessie could bounce herself from her toes to the top of a six story building but that sounds like exaggeration. She performeth at Weber & Fields' Music Hall."

No Foolin'

In the early 1900s, Bessie and Julian purchased five acres on Norwood Avenue in West Long Branch that included two mansions. Fans were shocked in 1910 when Bessie filed for a divorce. She toured Europe for a few years while her mother cared for the Mitchell's only child, Priscilla. Oddly, Bessie and Julian were estranged but lived in separate houses on the Norwood Avenue property until the divorce was finalized in 1923. Bessie retired from the stage and remarried.

While working as assistant director of Ziegfeld's 1926 show titled *No Foolin'*, Julian Mitchell became ill and died on the show's opening night. Bessie continued to reside at the Norwood Avenue estate. An accomplished equestrienne, Priscilla married Roger Pryor, the younger son of famous bandleader Arthur Pryor in 1926, the same year that her father died and left everything he had to her. Priscilla and Pryor lived at the Norwood Avenue property until 1934. Both of them would remarry. Bessie died in 1948 while living at Norwood Avenue with her granddaughter, aslo named Priscilla.

Celebrating Broadway

In 1950, Henry J. Shaheen, who was a mayor of West Long Branch, purchased the Mitchell mansion where he and wife would raise their children. In May 1999, the Mitchell mansion at 344 Norwood Avenue was the site of a Junior League of Monmouth County's Designer Showhouse and Gardens appropriately called "A Celebration of Broadway."

The dazzling stars of the Mitchell family left their mark on New York's Broadway, in Monmouth County, and beyond.

A twenty-first century photo of the former estate of Julian Mitchell, director of Broadway fame, and dancer Bessie Clayton, shows the mansion at 344 Norwood Avenue, West Long Branch, as it appears from the street.

A Victorian Idol - Edwin Adams

A well-known heartthrob in the mid-nineteenth century, Edwin Adams is an obscure star today. His career was cut short by his untimely death from consumption (tuberculosis) at age forty-three. An early and significant member of the actor's colony at Long Branch, he was a fine classical actor and a close associate of Edwin Booth.

A Man of Many Roles

Edwin Adams was born in 1834 in Medford, Massachusetts, and his first big role was in 1853 when he appeared in "The Hunchback." *Brown's History of the American Stage* states that, "He has appeared in all the principal cities in this country as a star, and is one of the best light comedians on the stage." Adams was scheduled to appear at Ford's Theatre just two days after Lincoln's assassination.

Edwin Booth noticed Adams' acting ability and chose him to play Mercutio supporting Booth as Romeo for the opening performance of *Romeo and Juliet* at Booth's magnificent New York Theatre in 1869. But when he played Iago to Booth's Othello, he was put down by the drama critics Perhaps his best role, and the one that he is associated with the most, was that of Enoch Arden.

Adams met his lovely wife, Miss Mary Whitworth, while he was leading man at the Richmond theatre and she was a member of the company. Mary was a niece of Dan Gardener, a well-known early circus clown with whom she was very close. Mrs. Adams was described as a "beautiful young lady, a clever actress and graceful *danseuse*" who retired from the stage at a young age, in the late 1860s.

Standing behind actress Kate Bateman, from left to right, are actors Edwin Adams, James Wallack Jr. and Joe Cowell, Bateman's grandfather. This 1862 carte de visite is the work of famous photographer Fredericks of New York who also had a Long Branch studio. Both Adams and Wallack owned homes at the Long Branch actors' colony.

The Adams' Cottage

The Adams' charming summer home, which appears on an 1873 map at the Northwest corner of Park Ave. and Deal Turnpike (Norwood Ave.), was called "Sea View." A photo by photographer Gustavus Pach and description of the house appear in Schenck's 1868 *Album of Long Branch*. Author Schenck points out that Adams' "romantic cottage" is hard to see from the road because of the shrubbery and trees:

"The designation is well chosen. The tower rises commandingly, the full size of an ordinary room. From its summit the range of view takes in the Ocean with the hotels and cottages upon the beach, and the Highlands in the distance. The house, with eight acres of ground (a portion of the Wooley farm) was bought of Mrs. W.R. Blake, in 1863 by Mr. Adams who has since added twenty-one acres, purchased of Allen Jeffrey."

This date, 1863, before McVicker bought his land in 1867, establishes Adams as one of the first actors to buy property in the area soon to be known as the actor's colony at Elberon. Perhaps he spread the word to his friends and associates, that the area was delightfully rural, yet close to the bustling activity of the oceanfront.

This unusual looking cottage with an "observatory" was the residence of Victorian idol Edwin Adams and his wife. It stood at the northwest corner of what is now Norwood and Park Avenues. From Schenck's *Album of Long Branch*, 1868. *Moss Archives*.

The comments written in Schenck's book about the house being difficult to see from the road with all the shrubs and trees give reason to believe that photographers, and perhaps fans, were trying to get a peek at the Adams' house in the summer. An article in The *Long Branch Daily News*, August 16, 1867, describes Gustavus Pach's latest photographic studio. Among the featured photos on display is a large print of the Edwin Adams' residence that was "taken in winter, the foliage being quite dense at any other time; and is colored up to Nature; the old-fashioned galleries in the foreground and the new portion beyond, containing the large tower, form a fine tout ensemble, and do credit to the artist." The Pach photo of the house in Schenck's book may be the same print or one taken around the same time, as there are no leaves on the trees.

The Final Tour

Edwin Adams toured across America and to Australia. Unfortunately, he became ill while appearing at Melbourne and had to return to the United States. He died peacefully at the home of his wife's uncle, Dan. Gardener, in Philadelphia and was buried at the Mount Moriah Cemetery in a plot owned by The Actors' Order of Friendship, as per his wishes. The handsome actor's untimely death shocked his fans. An obituary stated, "He was a man of fine personal presence, of generous and kindly nature with hosts of warm friends."

The residents of the Long Branch actors' colony greatly missed one of their founders and favorite neighbors. The original Adams house no longer stands.

Family Ties – The Wallacks

When he returned to his Long Branch home, actor Lester Wallack wore "a blue swallow-tail coat, with velvet collar and gilt buttons, a white vest, with rich fancy buttons, black knee breeches, and black silk stocking and pumps with delicate silver buckles...the correct thing for full dress, and as worn by Mr. Wallack, it is a very elegant costume." *The Long Branch News* 1869

Theatrical Cousins

While many stars of the Long Branch colony kept a low profile, the Wallacks seemed to enjoy being noticed. They were some of the earliest actors to invest in Long Branch property, possibly as far back as the 1850s. James W. Wallack (1818-1873) and his older brother Henry (1790-1870) were born to a theatrical family in England and established themselves as actors before relocating permanently to New York, but Henry never became as well known as his brother James W. Wallack.

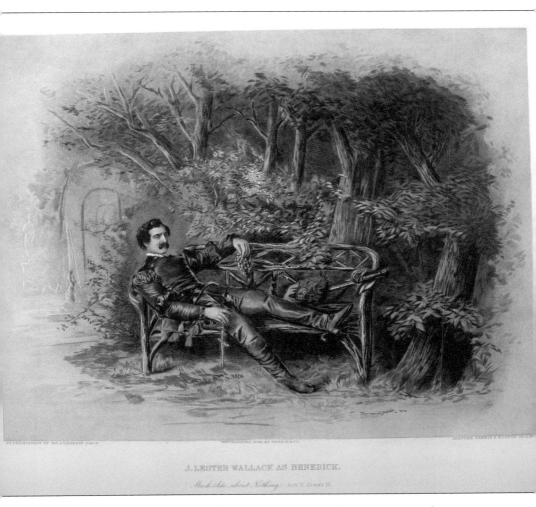

J. LESTER WALLACK AS BENEDICK.

Much Ado about Nothing ACT II. SCENE III.

An 1880s gravure print of J. Lester Wallack as Benedick in Shakespeare's *Much Ado About Nothing*, Act II, Scene III, in a reclining pose. Offstage, Wallack and his family relaxed at their well-appointed cottage at Long Branch.

Known as "the younger," Henry's son James W. Wallack Jr. (1818-1873) was born in London but came to America as a child. He spent much of his career touring the country while his cousin, Lester (John Johnstone) Wallack (1819-1888), the son of James W., became a well known actor and theater manager in New York. The cousins were both exceptionally handsome and well-liked. Described by a contemporary as "tall, straight as an Indian, graceful and distinguished in appearance," Lester played in hundreds of classical roles and in light comedy until his popularity waned in the 1870s.

By The Shores of Takanassee

Takanassee Lake, once a marshy area known as Green's Pond, was even called Wallack's Pond in the days when the Wallack family of actors owned homes at Long Branch. No wonder, as Wallacks were said to have made sure the pond was stocked with perch and pike for the pleasure of their friends who liked to fish. The charming cottage on the property belonging to James W. Jr., built in 1857 was called "Hopefield" and later known as "The Sycamores."

"The Hut" looks more like a mansion than a hut! Nevertheless that is what J. Lester Wallack called his cottage that was near Matilda Terrace. From Schenck's *Album of Long Branch. Moss Archives.*

Lester Wallack's land included several lots located west of Second Ave., opposite Matilda's Terrace. Around 1866, he built a large home opposite the Howland Hotel that he called "The Hut."

Water, Water, Everywhere

In 1867, Lester Wallack, concerned about improving the community, was one of the incorporators of the first water company at Long Branch. Takanasee Lake was purchased for a reservoir in 1874, but tap water was not available until 1878, first at the hotels and cottages and then at smaller homes.[1]

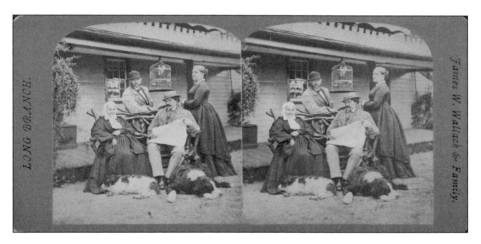

A stereograph of "J.W. Wallack and Family" taken by G.W. Pach in the late 1860s gives a casual look at the well-liked theatrical folk and their beloved pets at Long Branch. Actor James W. Wallack, Jr. is the man reading the paper. The photo was taken at his Long Branch home "Hopefield." This view and similar ones have also been titled "J.W. Wallack and friends." (Note: For several versions of this photo and more details see *Double Exposure Two* by Moss.)

Out for A Drive

Mrs. Lester Wallack, a sister of the well-known English artist, John Everett Millais, was a lady of fashion who wore the latest designer clothes. She and her husband had three sons and a daughter. Like many of the celebrities at Long Branch, the Wallacks were often seen driving their stylish carriages. The gossip column of *The Stage* for July 15, 1869, reported:

"The season is progressing finely at Long Branch, and the arrivals increase daily. Mr. Arthur Wallack drives a handsome trotter down the rotten row of Long Branch beach. He inherits the manly beauty of his father (Lester Wallack), somewhat softened by the poetic dreaminess of his mothers' look."

J.W. Wallack's Elberon home, "Hopefield," was a sprawling farmhouse located in the vicinity of Green's Pond that was sometimes called Wallack's Pond and is now known as Lake Takanassee.

Moving Uptown

James Wallack Sr.'s first New York theatre moved from lower Manhattan to further uptown at Broadway and 13th St. in 1861. Then his son Lester Wallack moved it up even further in 1881 to open the third Wallack's Theatre at 30th St. known as "The Germania" and then the "Star." It was torn down in 1901.

Hooray for Hollywood

An English actress from Liverpool named Josephine Shaw, a favorite leading lady of the Wallacks, came to America and made her American debut in 1839. Her second marriage was to John Hoey, a penniless Irish immigrant who worked his way up to become the head of the Adams Express Company. Upon her marriage to the wealthy Hoey, Josephine retired from acting, but James Wallack, Sr. convinced her to return to the stage in 1854.

Mr. and Mrs. Hoey visited the Wallack family at Long Branch and were so impressed that in 1859, they bought a farm on the south side of Cedar Ave. They spent a few summers there until they acquired a large parcel of land from H.S. Green on the north side of Cedar Ave. It was here that John Hoey transformed his brambly expanse of land with wild berry bushes and holly trees into an exquisite private park with formal gardens resembling oriental carpets, statuary, and hothouses full of tropical plants and exotic orchids. He called the place "Holly Wood." The Hoeys loved to entertain and in 1882, they capitalized on their popularity by building cottages that were expanded to become the Hollywood Hotel. However, in 1865, well before the Hoey's hotel, Mrs. Hoey had a quarrel with the Wallacks and retired permanently from the stage. But, eventually another actress would join the family when the Hoey's son Fred, who managed the hotel, married stage star Elsie Ferguson in August, 1907, at Christ Church in Shrewsbury.[2]

In another charming 1860s Wallack family portrait, actor James W., Jr. can be identified as the man standing. The woman and two little boys are most likely his wife and children. The man seated appears to be his uncle, actor James Wallack, Sr. The well-dressed Wallacks look like the very model of Victorian domestic tranquility.

Good Neighbors

The Wallacks represent important figures of the American theater who contributed to the early development of West End (Long Branch). Though many Victorians feared living next door to scandalous theatre folk, the fashionable Wallack families showed that theatrical stars could make good neighbors.

An Actor's Nest – Frank Chanfrau

In 1848, a streetwise-looking young man wearing a red flannel shirt, tightly fitting trousers and black boots was relaxing in the green room of downtown New York's Olympic Theatre. Shortly before the show was to begin, the theatre manager spotted him and "took him for a real fireman who had intruded himself behind the scenes and asked him what he wanted there."[1] It turned out that the handsome man was an actor waiting to go on stage. His name was Frank Chanfrau and he was realistically dressed as Mose, a nineteenth century New York volunteer fire fighter.

A Legendary Firefighter

The larger-than-life Mose character who could be compared to Paul Bunyan was based on a real man named Mose Humphreys who worked as a printer at *The New York Sun*. Humphreys was a volunteer rope man with Engine Co. No. 40. It was during the era of violent conflicts between street gangs in the Bowery and Five Points section of Manhattan. Frank Chanfrau's brother Henry was said to have defeated Mose in a fight in 1838, driving him out of the City. When Frank Chanfrau appeared as Mose in *A Glance at New York*, the raucous audience would cheer as soon as the character swaggered onstage, his soap locks partially covered by his stovepipe hat, his fireman's coat thrown over one arm and the stub of a cigar in his hand. However, not everyone was thrilled. It is said that some firemen were displeased with Chanfrau's portrayal that stereotyped the hard working fireman. Nevertheless, the play remained popular with the public mainly because of Chanfrau's charisma. It was rewritten to focus even more on Mose and the title was changed to *New York As It Is* and toured widely, making a hit with working class America, but a not so successful run in London. There were sequels including *Mose in California, Mose in China* and *Mose in a Muss* but they never equaled the popularity of the original.

A Gifted Impressionist

Francis "Frank" S. Chanfrau, actor and theatrical manager, was born to French parents in New York City in 1824.

THE AMERICAN ON THE STAGE.

MR. F. S. CHANFRAU AS "MOSE." (BY PERMISSION, AFTER LITHOGRAPH DRAWN BY JAMES BROWN.)

"The American on the Stage," *Scribner's Monthly*, July 1879, included this illustration by James Brown of "Mr. F.S. Chanfrau as Mose." The legendary hero was based on a real mid-nineteenth century New York Bowery volunteer fire fighter. Actor Frank S. Chanfrau and his wife owned a good deal of land in Monmouth County.

When he was young, he saw a performance by the great actor Edwin Forrest and knew that he wanted to become an actor too. He had a gift for imitating ethnic speech and doing impersonations. He even impersonated Edwin Forrest. There exist several stories as to how

Frank Chanfrau took to speaking in the Irish brogue of the Bowery's "b'hoys." In any case, he was convincing.

The Cozy Nest

Performing was tough work and actors who often did two shows a day needed to get away whenever possible. The countryside to the west of Long Branch, close to the sea and yet far enough from the crowded Bowery, appealed to Frank Chanfrau and his wife. Both thespians working in New York, Mr. and Mrs. Chanfrau were two of the first players to live in the area that would become known as the Long Branch Actors' Colony. Henrietta Baker Chanfrau had starred as Portia in the famous production of Julius Caesar in 1864, the only time that the three Booth brothers appeared together.

Around 1870, Frank and Henrietta Chanfrau purchased a tranquil twenty-acre farm in what is now West Long Branch. Their house, affectionately called "The Nest" was located at the corner of Cedar and Elmwood Avenues. Although originally a simple farmhouse, it was quite large, well furnished, and included rooms for servants.

"The Nest," Mr. and Mrs. Frank Chanfrau's comfortable farmhouse on Cedar Ave. (now West Long Branch) was photographed by G.W. Pach for Schenck's *Album of Long Branch*, 1868. Chanfrau also owned oceanfront property at Elberon and intended to build a more elaborate house there but apparently never did. *Moss Archives.*

Changing With the Times

Although Mose was well-liked for years, the popularity of the character began to diminish as New York City grew and professional firefighters replaced volunteers. And Chanfrau was getting too old to play the athletic hunk Mose. He became the manager of a New York theater and eventually developed other popular characters, including the title role in *Kit the Arkansas Traveler*.

Frank Chanfrau died in Jersey City, on October 2, 1884. His wife Henrietta remained in the Long Branch area. In 1888, Mrs. Chanfrau sold their property to New York publisher Norman L. Munro and most of it would become part of his cottage community, Norwood Park. The Chanfrau house, "The Nest," survived until a very cold winter day in 1965 when it burned to the ground.

A Tall Tale

Frank Chanfrau's name may not be recognized today, but the character of Mose that he popularized became known again after Herbert Asbury's 1920s book *The Gangs of New York*. Mose has become a "tall tale" folk hero in modern anthologies. Since the exceptional bravery of New York City firefighters on September 11, 2001, the legend of Mose has been revised and retold again in several books for children.

The Fairy Princess – Mary Anderson

"At the Branch is an actress named Mary
Who's as fresh as new milk from the dairy
When she rides all the beaux get up on tip toes
And swear she's as trim as a fairy."
By an anonymous fan,
printed in the *Long Branch News*, c. 1880s [1]

Whenever Mary Anderson appeared in public, admirers jockeyed to get a peek at the young actress whose looks enchanted many an eligible bachelor. Although known to be a summer resident of the Long Branch actors' colony in the early 1880s, few records are available about her activities there as she most likely wanted privacy. But she was often spotted in a carriage enjoying her afternoon "gallop" in the countryside.

A Blossoming Career

Mary was born in Sacramento, California, in 1859 but raised in Louisville, Kentucky, where she began acting and made her stage debut at the age of sixteen as Juliet. It is said that she wanted to go into acting after seeing Edwin Adams act in *The Hunchback*. Mary's father, a Confederate soldier, died in 1863 when she was only four years old. When she was eight, her widowed mother married Dr. Hamilton Griffin, of Louisville, who had served as a Confederate Army doctor. It is said that Griffin encouraged his step-daughter's theatrical career and helped her to get acting and elocution lessons.

Besides classic beauty, she had great talent. Her career blossomed quickly and she became well loved across America. In 1883, Mary debuted in London with huge success but returned home in the mid 1880s to perform in New York.

Mary's Family at Long Branch

Mary Anderson reportedly first summered at Long Branch in 1878 at the age of nineteen, and in 1880, she stayed at a summer cottage on the northwest corner of Cedar and South St. (now Norwood Avenue), slightly west of Hoey's "Holly Wood" estate. The home that belonged to Chicago theatrical entrepreneur Matt Canning was acquired by Mary's stepfather Dr. Griffin around 1879. The 1880 census shows Anderson's entire family living there: Dr. Hamilton Griffin, 47; his wife (Mary's mother) Antonia, 46; Mary Anderson, 20; Charles Anderson, 17; three Griffin children, ages 12, 8, and 4; a coachman, a maid, and an Irish actor named Robert Bourne. Dr. Griffin's occupation is listed as "Theatrical Manager" and Mary's brother Charles is listed as an actor. It appears that Dr. Griffin was his stepdaughter's manager. Mary's brother apparently did not become well known, and the presence of the Irish born actor is a mystery although he did appear in some plays with Mary.

The classical profile of Mary Anderson in 1875 at the age of sixteen. From her autobiography, *A Few Memories*, published in 1896. She summered at Long Branch.

Norman Munro and Norwood Park

In 1886, the Griffin family sold the property and the house that was called "The Mary Anderson Cottage" to the affluent New York dime novel publisher, Norman L. Munro. An avid enthusiast of steam powered yachts, Munro wanted to be near but not directly on the water. He lived in the Anderson cottage for a season but the following year, he had it moved to the rear of his property and a mansion built on its former site. He named his grand new home "Normahurst."[2]

On the surrounding property, Munro built a complex of cottages known as Norwood Park that included a small casino where well-known performers would entertain the guests. After Munro died in 1894, his widow Henrietta retained the property but leased it when she would often travel abroad. Vice-president during McKinley's administration, Garret A. Hobart (1844-1899) was born in West Long Branch. He rented Normahurst in 1899 when he was in ill health. The Munro mansion was destroyed by fire in 1902 and on its site in 1905, the new owner, Murry Guggenheim, built a splendid new mansion that is now The Murry and Leonie Guggenheim Memorial Library of Monmouth University. Some of the Norwood Park cottages remain today.

An early twentieth century postcard shows the Murry Guggenheim Cottage built in 1905 that became the Murry and Leonie Guggenheim Memorial Library of Monmouth University on Cedar Ave. in West Long Branch. A home owned by publisher Norman Munro that burned down was previously on the site and before that it was the location of actress Mary Anderson's house.

But What About Mary?

In 1887, Mary Anderson returned to London and became the first actress to play both Perdita and Hermione in *The Winter's Tale*. The play was so well liked that she brought the production to the United States the following year. But soon after that, she suffered from nervous exhaustion and collapsed during a performance in 1889.

Much to the dismay of her fans, she decided to give up her theatrical career. Perhaps it was a matter of too much too soon. Returning to England, she married Antonio de Navarro and retired from the stage at the age of thirty.

With no regrets about her decision, Mary Anderson de Navarro lived a good life in England with her husband and two children. She published an autobiography, *A Few Memories*, in 1896, stating in the introduction that she wanted to make young women aware of the difficulties and dangers of a theatrical career. She did some volunteer work and appearances during World War I, but never returned to

acting as a profession. In 1936, she wrote another book called *A Few More Memories*.

She died in 1940 at her home in Worcestershire, England at the age of eighty-one. Despite her early retirement, she is still remembered as one of the most beautiful and talented classical stars ever to grace the stage.

An English cabinet photo of Mary Anderson as Perdita in Shakespeare's *The Winter's Tale* in January 1889 accentuates the alluring charm of the American born actress in one of her final roles. She retired from the stage at the age of thirty, got married, and lived the rest of her life in England.

A lovely photo by W. and D. Downey of London as seen on a Rotary Series Photographic postcard from the early 1900s shows Mary Anderson deep in thought as she reads.

The Jersey Lily – Lillie Langtry

Which Jersey was that?

When Lillie Langtry (1852-1929), known as "The Jersey Lily," visited the New Jersey shore in the 1880s, vacationers and residents scrambled to get a peek at the scandalous international beauty. (Her nickname had nothing to do with New Jersey.) The British actress with the peaches 'n cream complexion was born on the Isle of Jersey in 1853 and christened Emilie Charlotte Le Breton. The only daughter of a clergyman, she had six brothers. In 1874, she married Edward Langtry, an Irish property-owner.

A portrait of Lillie Langtry by Burr McIntosh that was made into a postcard for the early twentieth century "Rotograph" series. "The Jersey Lily" was fittingly posed by vases of lilies. The English star was a much talked about visitor to the Monmouth County Shore.

Supposedly, young Emilie fell for him because of his impressive yacht and wanted him to take her away from the country life of the Channel Islands. They didn't travel far, but they did move to London where Emilie hoped to establish herself as a society wife.

But their life was not as comfortable as she had expected it to be. Edward soon went bankrupt, the marriage failed, and Emilie found herself penniless and in debt. Nevertheless, her remarkable charm had not gone unnoticed by Londoners. Artists wanted to paint her because of her classical Grecian looking features. She was already well known as a society beauty when she decided to take up acting and made her theater debut in 1881.

The Unfaithful Lily

Now using the name "Lillie Langtry," the exquisite beauty from Jersey was a hit on stage, especially with the adoring gentlemen fans. Though still married, she carried on scandalous affairs with prominent men. She gave birth to a baby girl named Jeanne Marie Langtry the same year she started working in the theater. There are several theories as to who the child's father was, but it was probably not Edward Langtry. The most likely father was Prince Louis of Battenberg, one of Lillie's lovers and the father of Lord Mountbatten. Without question, the most noteworthy of Lillie's affairs was her relationship with Queen Victoria's son, Albert Edward, known as "Bertie," who would become King Edward VII. She was quite openly accepted as the Prince's mistress.

A cabinet photo of English superstar Lillie Langtry shows her in what was considered a rather seductive pose in the 1880s. She was well known on both sides of the Atlantic and photos like this were sold to fans. Although she also posed for famous American theatrical photographers, this image is by Lafayette of Dublin, who was well known for his portraits of royalty.

Lillie's Friends

The adventurous Lillie, at the suggestion of her Irish author friend, Oscar Wilde, decided to visit America in 1882-83. Wilde, a leader of the aesthetic movement, was already in the States on a lecture tour when Lillie arrived. She was also close friends with the painter James McNeill Whistler, who she met in England. It was an exciting era when many artists and performers were commuting back and forth between Europe and the States. The American public was very excited about the coming of foreign stars and their tours were highly publicized.

Upon his arrival in New York in 1882, Irish wit Oscar Wilde had his photograph taken with grand flair to kick off a lecture tour that included Long Branch and other stops at the New Jersey Shore. For this portrait of the aesthetic author, Napoleon Sarony decided to pose his subject in a fabulous fur-trimmed coat creating an artistic and original work. It was Wilde who encouraged Lillie Langtry to visit America.

OSCAR WILDE.

Copyright 1882, by N. Sarony.

37 UNION SQR., N.Y.

Her Private Pullman Car

The charming Lillie acquired fans and lovers wherever she performed. In New York City, she met a wealthy local playboy named Freddie Gebhard. He worshipped her and presented her with extravagant gifts including a plush Pullman railroad car named "Lalee." Freddie's father came from a family of New York merchants and his mother's family owned real estate in New York and New Jersey. Although the fun-loving Freddie apparently did not hold a "regular" job, he bred thoroughbred horses for a while and was said to be well known at the racetracks including Monmouth Park.

An amusing drawing from a vintage newspaper shows the shapely "daughter of one of the aristocratic cottagers" balanced on a man's shoulders, trying to peek at Lillie Langtry through a window of her private rail car, the "Lalee." Lillie's boyfriend, Freddie Gebhard, is on the rear platform, trying to shoo the celebrity seekers away.

Numerous sensationalized stories appeared in the press about Lillie's escapades at the New Jersey shore. Victorians had a ravenous appetite for gossip, just as many people today read the tabloids or watch television talk shows. On one of Lillie and Freddie's jaunts to Long Branch on the "Lalee," the luxurious train car was said to be pulled over to rest on a side track at Third and Bath Avenues where the couple planned to spend a few secluded days together. As things turned out, they had no privacy as people gathered around the car trying to steal a look at them.

The Water Lily

Other remarkable stories about The Jersey Lily at Long Branch depict her as "The Water Lily" when she shocked beachgoers by bathing in a "revealing," form-fitting costume with bare arms, no stockings and a rather low-cut bodice. Another tale recounts how Lillie went bathing in the nude at Pleasure Bay, where she was spotted by a *New York Herald Tribune* reporter. Yet another news item reported that Lillie was drinking in public at the bar of the United States Hotel with

Freddie (something ladies did not do)! The couple were said to frequent the races at Monmouth Park and to dine afterward at Price's Pleasure Bay Hotel.

Her New Jersey Homes

There seem to be different reports as to exactly where Lillie stayed in Long Branch, as she apparently rented several different cottages at various times. Some sources say that she used the Park Wooley house at 127 Bath Avenue during 1888 and 1889. Others state that she rented the George W. Brown cottage at Bath and Sairs Avenues, that later became a nurses' residence for Monmouth Medical Center. Lillie is also said to have lived with a theatrical family on Atlantic Avenue in North Long Branch at first, and then moved into one of the twin cottages belonging to Phil Daly on the northeast corner of Second and Chelsea Avenues. "Daly built the ornate houses after he successfully bet $50,000 on Grover Cleveland to win in the election of 1892. Naming the houses *The Phil* and *The Catherine*, for his wife, Daly liked to boast that 'President Cleveland gave me those two houses.' During the summer that Mrs. Langtry lived in *The Catherine*, she kept her private car (the "Lalee") on a railroad siding.[1]

Another cartoon of Lillie Langtry that hit the newspapers while she was touring the United States in 1883 depicts her in a "risqué" bathing costume in the Long Branch surf. The bluff by the West End Hotel is in the background and the well-dressed gent on the shore is most likely her beau, Freddie Gebhard.

The Western Lily

In 1887, Lillie divorced her husband. She went with Freddie to live in California, where she purchased some 4,600 acres of Guenoc Valley land, about ninety miles north of San Francisco. There, she and Freddie could breed horses and Lillie started a winery. She even brought an expert vintner from Bordeaux, France, to help. The actress placed her own portrait on the wine bottle labels.[2]

One of Lillie's most celebrated admirers was Judge Roy Bean, the legendary Texas frontier judge (immortalized in the movies). He practiced his outrageous type of justice at a small tent city already called "Langtry" for a railroad boss by that name, but Bean insisted he had named it for Lillie. Although he never met her, the eccentric Bean was infatuated with Lillie and built a saloon that he called "The Jersey Lily." Lillie corresponded with him but never met her Texas admirer. She visited Langtry city about ten months after Judge Bean's death in 1903.

An Everlasting Lily

The Jersey Lily was often seen in print advertisements for Pear's soap, and is said to be one of the first women to be paid for endorsements of commercial products. In 1889, Lillie married Hugo Gerald de Bathe, who was considerably younger than she. He became a baron and owned race horses. De Bathe and Lillie retired to Monte Carlo, where she died in 1929. She is buried on the Isle of Jersey, in the graveyard of St. Savior's church where her father had been the vicar. Lillie has been the subject of many books, films, and a PBS television series made in the 1970s. Wherever she went, including the Monmouth County shore, The Jersey Lily caused a sensation. She is a superstar of yesteryear with a name that is well recognized even today.

Beauty and the Gourmand – Lillian Russell and Diamond Jim Brady

"Nothing can make one beautiful. No one can make one beautiful. Beauty is the outward expression of inner excellence." From "Reminiscences" by Lillian Russell, *Cosmopolitan*, May 1922.

The name Lillian Russell, the glam star with an hour glass shape, invariably turns up in publications about the history of New Jersey shore. The buxom Lillian, wearing a huge ostrich plume hat, and her frequent escort, portly "Diamond Jim" Brady, have become symbols of the high life in late nineteenth century America.

Of course, there existed a down side to that period of time. Poverty, political unrest, bigotry, disease, and crime – all of these problems plagued the nation, yet the era seems to be recalled more often for its romantic aspects. Despite her outward appearance and luxurious taste, Lillian Russell was socially conscious and crusaded for women's suffrage.

This stunning portrait of singing star Lillian Russell in a stylish ostrich plume hat was taken by Pach Brothers' New York studio where they photographed hundreds of celebrities. The photo appears on a "Rotograph" series postcard, dated 1907.

Lillian and Diamond Jim regularly visited the New Jersey shore, but were also spotted at dozens of resorts up and down the East coast, including Atlantic City. At Monmouth County, they frequented the boardwalks, Monmouth Park racetrack, Price's restaurant at Pleasure Bay, and the Hollywood Hotel. Lillian occasionally visited friends in Little Silver, including Richard K. Fox, publisher of the infamous *Police Gazette*, and his family at their estate, Fox Hill.

That Little Girl from Iowa

Born Helen Louise Leonard, in 1861 at Clinton, Iowa, Lillian's father was the owner and editor of the local newspaper and her mother was a staunch supporter of the women's suffrage movement. The family moved to Chicago where Lillian studied before she made her New York stage debut at the age of eighteen in the chorus of Gilbert and Sullivan's *H.M.S. Pinafore*.

She was soon discovered by New York vaudeville producer Tony Pastor, who gave her the stage name of "Lillian Russell." He put her in his revues where she belted out English music hall favorites during the 1880s. By the

A rare 1880s cabinet photo by Anderson shows Lillian Russell in her slim, early days. Lillian is most likely in costume for the opera bouffe, *Olivette*, in which she played a cabin boy who sings "In the North Sea Lived a Whale" and dances the hornpipe. One of the first times that Diamond Jim laid eyes on Lillian was when she appeared in this role.

"gay nineties," the name of this blue-eyed blonde with the ample figure was a household word, as she appeared in dozens of popular musicals and comic operas. Shows were even written especially for her, including *Polly* (1885), *La Cigale* (1891), and *An American Beauty*

(1896). She joined the great Weber and Fields team, and in their production of *Twirly-Whirly* she sang her famous number, "Come Down, Ma Evenin' Star," the only song she ever recorded.

All That Sparkles...And All You Can Eat

A business man, not an actor, Diamond Jim Brady was a real-life showman who didn't hesitate to flash his sparkly stickpins, cuflinks, and rings. He even owned a "transportation" set of diamond jewelry in the shapes of various vehicles. Born in New York, James Buchanan Brady, the son of an Irish immigrant saloon keeper, worked his way up from bellhop, to baggage handler, to ticket agent, to salesman of railroad supplies, to wealthy financier.

Known as a superior "gourmand," Brady's appetite was astounding. Lillian would join him in his famous repasts and eat heartily, though certainly not as much as Diamond Jim! Typically, Brady would consume dozens of oysters, crabs, and tureens of turtle soup followed by steaks, chops, fowl, and potatoes. Then, for dessert, he devoured pastries and chocolates. Although he liked gourmet food, he didn't drink any wine or alcohol. He washed his huge meal down with a quart or two of his favorite beverage, that he called "golden nectar" – straight orange juice.

Horseless Carriages

Besides good eats, sparkly jewels, and beautiful women, Diamond Jim also found the new fangled "horseless carriage" to be of interest. He and Lillian got into the 1890s bicycling craze (perhaps in an attempt to take off some pounds after those huge meals)!

James Buchanan Brady

"God, Nell, ain't it grand!" This quote by Diamond Jim Brady reflects the lifestyle of Lillian Russell's frequent escort who is pictured here, c.1890s. (Lillian was called "Nell.") The wealthy businessman consumed "super size" gourmet meals and flaunted his custom-made diamond jewelry.

Jim had a gold-plated, jeweled bike designed for Lillian, but automobiles were even more appealing. He is said to have owned the first electric auto in New York City. He purchased not one, but six automobiles and hired a chauffeur for each of them. One auto, designed to Brady's specifications, cruised down Ocean Avenue in Long Branch, with Diamond Jim and Lillian riding inside.[1] They were probably dressed to the nines and caused quite a sensation. However, most of Brady's motoring was done in New York City at his main residence, where he garaged his cars.

A Poet's View

Although they fre-
quented many resorts,
Long Branch claims a spe-
cial affection for the legendary duo of Lillian and
Diamond Jim that cannot
be denied. Unfortunately,
no photographic images
are known to have sur-
vived of the pair together.
A native of Long Branch,
the renowned poet, essay-

A 1907 postcard from a series published by Raphael Tuck & Sons depicts people strolling, horse drawn carriages, and a lone automobile on Ocean Ave., Long Branch, a symbol of changing times and evocative of Lillian and Diamond Jim's ride.

ist, and educator, Robert Pinsky (United States poet laureate from 1997-2000), writes:

> "In Long Branch, the sporting figure of Diamond Jim Brady entertained Lillian Russell, gliding along the ocean at dusk in an early electric auto-mobile, the crystal passenger compartment illuminated and the chauffeur in darkness, so that the large-bodied, extravagantly draperied and tailored lovers could be seen as though in a moving department store window. Be-hind them, a noiseless parade of three spare vehicles in case the main one failed, each with its driver."[2]

Relationships

Lillian was married four times. Her husbands were Harry Braham, Edward Solomon, both musical directors; Giovanni Perugini, an Italian tenor; and Edward Moore, a publisher. She had a son who died as an infant and a daughter who survived her. Brady remained a bachelor all his life.

In 1906, Diamond Jim purchased a house and farm "on the Raritan River, near Somerville"[3] It later became a hotel. Jim would entertain friends and clients there. He was enamored with a shop girl named Edna McCauley, and was said to rent a cottage in Belmar for the two of them one season. But Edna fell in love with copper magnate Jesse Lewisohn, whom Lillian had been interested in. The four of them spent many good times together. Then, Edna and Jesse got married and Lillian and Diamond Jim remained close companions.

Diamonds in the Sky

Brady died in Atlantic City from kidney disease and diabetes in 1917, at the age of sixty-one. In her final years, Lillian Russell spent most of her time writing, crusading for women's rights, and doing philanthropic work. She died in 1922, shortly before her sixty-first birthday.

Wherever they went, the glittering duo attracted attention. Like diamonds in the sky...Lillian and Diamond Jim still sparkle!

Act II
North Long Branch
and Monmouth Beach

Besides Elberon and the rustic area to its west, Victorian theatrical stars found North Long Branch, the northernmost section of coastal Long Branch, a desirable place to live. The thespians were also attracted to the cottage life at Monmouth Beach, a town adjacent to North Long Branch and home to an early life saving station (now a cultural center). These areas that were also known for commercial fishing experienced an increase in summer visitors with the coming of the railroad in the mid-nineteenth century.

Wild West Showman –
Nate Salsbury

"A Globe Trotter's Tribute to Long Branch – I have seen all the boosted watering resorts of the world and I can assure you that nowhere is there a stretch of country that can compare with the territory between Monmouth Beach and Deal." Nate Salsbury (from a 1907 Long Branch souvenir view book)

Never in buckskins, Nate Salsbury the co-owner and master mind of Buffalo Bill's Wild West was always dressed like a gentleman. The well-respected Long Branch resident is seen here looking trim in a suit and top hat when he took the show to London in 1891. *Denver Public Library, Western History Collection, N-62.*

In the late nineteenth century, actor and producer Nate Salsbury's name was well recognized, although he never reached the superstar status of his business partner, William F. "Buffalo Bill" Cody. Salsbury masterminded one of the most successful entertainments of his day, Buffalo Bill's Wild West.

Already a well-known actor and show business entrepreneur, Salsbury became Cody's business partner and co-owner of Buffalo Bill's Wild West in 1883. Cody attained status as an American legend for his real life roles as buffalo hunter and U.S. Army Scout. Few people today know much about Nate Salsbury, and even fewer know of his strong connections to Long Branch, New Jersey, in the latter part of his life. Much of the business of Buffalo Bill's Wild West was conducted in Long Branch by Salsbury who liked the city so much that he settled there with his family in the 1890s. He purchased a house on Liberty Street, and became a vital figure in the community. Contrary to popular belief, Cody did not live in or own property at Long Branch although he did visit the area.

Nate's Early Years

Nathan "Nate" Salsbury was born in Rockford, Illinois, in 1845. He was orphaned at the age of eight and, when sixteen, he ran off to join the Union Army as a drummer boy. Energetic young Nate entertained the troops by singing and dancing. Besides his theatrical ability, Salsbury allegedly exhibited a remarkable talent for playing poker. After the war, he is said to have left the army with $20,000 in winnings from card games.

Salsbury began to study finance and law, but soon ran out of money and decided to look for a career in the theater. He loved to act but had no formal training. He landed a part in the play "Pocohontas" at a Michigan theater, but the show closed after just one performance! Salsbury kept plugging away at acting despite hard times with itinerant companies in the late 1860s and early 1870s. Then, he took a job as a comedian at the celebrated Boston Museum (a theatre) in Massachuestts, and stayed for four years.

After gaining experience in Boston, Salsbury decided to start his own stock company and named the group The Salsbury Troubadours. His little ensemble was a smash hit and traveled for twelve years, including tours in Europe and Australia.

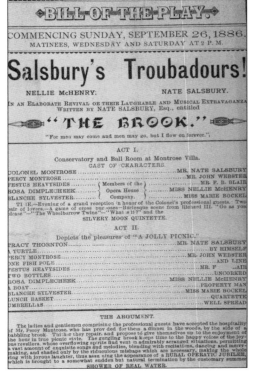

The Brook, Nate Salsbury's Troubadours famous comedy was about a picnic and includes "A Turtle" played "By Himself" in the cast list! The play is recognized as one of the first significant American musical comedies. This program is from 1886.

Salsbury Meets Cody

In 1883, while playing in Chicago with his Troubadours, Salsbury attended an arena performance that would change his life. After seeing Buffalo Bill Cody's western exhibition, that was on its first tour, Salsbury immediately purchased a sizeable interest in the show. He continued touring with his Troubadours to build up more capital and waited until Cody's business partner, Dr. William F. Carver, a sharp-shooting dentist known as "The Evil Spirit of the Plains," gave up and left the show. Salsbury could not have tolerated working with Carver who was considered to be hot-tempered and undependable.

Cody and Salsbury made an interesting team and seemed to have mutual respect for each other. Cody, the tall, rugged, former Indian scout, dressed the part of a flashy showman with his long flowing hair, cowboy hat, and fringe. Salsbury, small and thin, usually wearing a high silk hat or derby and tailcoat, gave the impression of a refined English aristocrat. The boisterous Cody and mild-mannered Salsbury complimented each other in a way that may have helped their business relationship to succeed. Cody didn't know much about finance, but Salsbury added structure to the show that was badly in need of financial organization. He is said to have helped keep Cody sober.

Little Sure Shot and Sitting Bull

The most significant performers that Salsbury hired for the Wild West were Annie Oakley and Chief Sitting Bull. "Little Sure Shot," as Annie was called, joined the show in April of 1885. Salsbury had no doubt that the attractive little sharpshooter, who originally hailed from Ohio, would be a big hit. Legend has it that Annie was invited in 1889 by Fred Hoey, of the Hollywood Hotel at Long Branch, to participate in a live-bird shooting match with Phil Daly, Jr. Although Daly was supposed to be the nation's best live-bird shot, Annie defeated him with ease and won a good wager. Allegedly, Annie loaned him the money a decade later when he needed it.[1]

"Little Sure Shot." This studio photograph of Annie Oakley was taken by photographer Barry in the 1890s. During this decade the shooting star of Buffalo Bill's Wild West and her husband Frank Butler lived in Nutley and would visit with Nate Salsbury and his family at Long Branch. *Denver Public Library, Western History Collection, B-941.*

Annie Oakley and her manager-husband, Frank Butler, did not live at Long Branch, but were New Jersey residents in the 1890s when they owned a house in Nutley and occasionally visited Long Branch. During this period, Annie and other Wild West performers appeared in a pioneer film made at the Edison studio in West Orange. Annie remained a close friend of the Salsbury family. It has been rumored that Annie and Frank first wanted to buy a house near the Hollywood Hotel at Long Branch, but decided on the Nutley house instead.

Sitting Bull, the illustrious Sioux chief with a firm jaw and weathered face, is associated with Custer's Last Stand. Sitting Bull was hired by Salsbury for the Wild West show just two months after Annie was hired. The audiences booed the Chief, as he was presented as a villain. In reality, the Sitting Bull was said to be a kind man who gave some of the money he earned from the show to orphans and waifs who he encountered while touring.

On Liberty Street

In 1886 at the age of forty-one, Nate Salsbury married Rachel "Rae" Samuels, who came from Brooklyn, New York. She had been one of his Troubadours. The couple apparently spent some summers at Long Branch hotels, enjoyed the place, and decided to settle there. Their house at 279 Liberty Street (replaced by another house many years ago) was purchased from Frank Maeder, another of Salsbury's Troubadours who became musical director of Buffalo Bill's Wild West. Nellie McHenry and her husband, John Webster, former members of the Troubadours, did not work with the Wild West show but lived in the Highlands Hills and remained friends of the Salsburys.

Nate and Rae Salsbury started a family and had four children, Nate Jr., Milton, and twin girls named Rachel and Rebecca.[2] Salsbury was comfortable and happy at his home on Troutman's Creek, just a few blocks from the Atlantic Ocean.

Meanwhile, Nate Salsbury continued his career adding more attractions to the Wild West show and booking tours. One of his brainstorms, the "Congress of the Rough Riders of the World," quickly became a popular feature. He brought in horseback riders from all over, including Cossacks from Russia and gauchos from South America. It was this extravaganza of foreign horsemanship that stirred Theodore Roosevelt's United States Army regiment of Volunteer Cavalry to be called the "Rough Riders."

In 1887, the Wild West troupe, under Salsbury's skillful management, embarked on their first tour to England. The trip was wildly successful with the British, and even Queen Victoria praised the troupe. The Wild West toured many other nations, including France, Germany, Spain, and Italy where Cody and some of the Native Americans posed for a publicity photo in a gondola at Venice.

Salsbury's Docudrama

Salsbury wanted the Wild West to be entertaining, but also insisted that it be a historical documentary and not merely a spectacle. In the days before movies and television, the public was excited to see re-creations of real events.

"All Roads Lead to…" Ambrose Park, South Brooklyn, was the site of Buffalo Bill's Wild West for the entire 1894 season. This marvelous lithograph poster with pictures of Cody and Salsbury gives an artistic bird's eye view of New York City and New Jersey. Notice the Statue of Liberty and The Brooklyn Bridge. *Buffalo Bill Historical Center; Cody; Wyoming, 1:69.20.*

The Wild West show was a far-cry from being accurate, and it presented a misleading version of Native Americans and life in the developing American West. It seems to have been Salsbury's intention to depict history truthfully, but not by losing the action and thrills needed to make a profit. In the late 1890s, Salsbury produced another historical show, an innovative musical with an all black cast, called Black America, in an endeavor to depict Afro-American history.

The Wild West show's reputation as a circus developed during the time that James Bailey, of Barnum and Bailey circus fame, took over as the manager of Buffalo Bill's Wild West in 1895, after Salsbury's health began to fail. But Salsbury remained the co-owner of the show and invested in mining in the West and real estate in the East.

The Reservation

By the late 1890s, Salsbury reportedly made around $40,000 a year and said that he "planned to spend every cent of it" in Long Branch.[3] Near the close of the century, at a sheriff's sale, Salsbury purchased the North Long Branch beachfront property known as the "East End tract" that had passed through several owners and once belonged to the infamous financier, Jay Gould. On the former site of the East End Hotel, Salsbury built nine grand cottages, each with separate stables nearby. Leon Cubberley was the architect. Salsbury remained at his Liberty Street house nearby, and did not live in the oceanfront houses; they were constructed as investment properties. Cody, contrary to popular belief, never lived in these buildings, although some performers may have occupied them at various times.

The group of cottages were called "The Reservation," because Salsbury named them out of respect for his Native American employees. The four houses along the one-thousand-foot beachfront (from north to south) were named Arapaho, Navaho, Iroquois, and Cheyenne. The five houses on what was then Ocean Drive were Shoshone, Okelsska, Cherokee, Okechobee, and Uncapaca. Between the two rows of homes there was a private road called 'The Trail," with an American flag waving proudly on a tall pole in the center.

The cottages were not as grand as some of those built in the area some ten to twenty years earlier; however, they were luxurious compared to the small bungalows constructed at that time. Modifications and modern improvements were made to the cottages over the years and their owners enjoyed the location. In the

A postcard, c. 1913, shows some houses that were part of "The Reservation" built by Nate Salsbury in 1900 at North Long Branch. It is said that Dick Foran (1910-1979), a matinee idol of Grade B Westerns who was born in New Jersey, lived in one of The Reservation houses.

early 1980s, despite controversy, most of The Reservation houses were razed and the 33-acre site became Seven Presidents Oceanfront Park, part of the Monmouth County Park System. Only one cottage remains that is used as an activity center for the park.

The Environmentalist

Nate Salsbury was ahead of his time in exhibiting concern for the environment. The showman's ideas, however, were apparently not scientific or even feasible. According to *Entertaining A Nation*, Salsbury planned "an outlet from the ocean to the Shrewsbury that would clean the river for fishing" and "to stimulate the river current by hundreds of glass mason jars filled with sea water."[4] The scheme was never executed.

The True Star

Nate Salsbury died on December 24, 1902, at his Liberty Street home. The Wild West show continued, but was never quite the same without Salsbury's creative and entrepreneurial skills. He was, unquestionably, the true Wild West star of the New Jersey shore.

A Foresighted Actor
and Cottager – Oliver Byron

"Without doubt the best known cottager along the North Jersey Coast is Oliver Byron. With Mrs. Byron he is occupying Castle Byron on Ocean Avenue, North Long Branch." *The Long Branch Daily Record*, August 2, 1902

Well-known actor Oliver Doud Byron and his wife, actress Mary Kate Crehan Byron, took a great interest in their community at the New Jersey Shore. The couple's home at 459 Ocean Avenue, North Long Branch, where they summered for almost fifty years was affectionately known as "Castle Byron." Though it was a splendid oceanfront cottage with fine furnishings, the house did not resemble a European palace. The locals referred to Byron as the "Summer Mayor," not as a king. All the same, he was admired, well-respected and influential.

Right:
In a portrait from an 1894 publication, actor and "summer mayor" of North Long Branch, Oliver Doud Byron, shows off his moustache and expressive eyebrows. Byron and his wife Kate acquired a great deal of property and built houses in the area, some of which still stand.

On the Right Track

Oliver Byron was born in Frederick, Maryland, in 1842. He made his acting debut, in Baltimore as Oliver B. Doud in 1856, appearing with the great actor, Joseph Jefferson. He played alongside John Wilkes Booth that same year in Virginia, toured the South, and then joined Wallack's Company in New York. For a while, he alternated in the roles of Iago and Othello with Edwin Booth. But Byron's greatest success was with melodramas that he produced and acted in, starting in the 1870s. In *Across the Continent*, that first opened in 1871, he played the hero, Joe Ferris, for over thirty years. Another sensationalized Byron show that audiences loved was *The Inside Track*. The characters in these plays were stereotypes and the adventurous plots provided escapist entertainment that made Byron both popular and wealthy.

A stunning late 19th century poster for one of Oliver Doud Byron's popular productions, *The Inside Track*. The sensational melodrama starring Oliver and Kate Byron claimed to have 'the most realistic fire scene ever produced!"

Three Sisters

Oliver and Mary Kate Crehan (usually called Kate) were married on November 23, 1869, and lived in Brooklyn. Kate came from an Irish immigrant family who had settled in Brooklyn. Kate and her sister, Hattie, were already in the theater when Ada, their younger sister, decided she wanted to become an actress, too. Due to a typographical error on an early program, her name was listed as "Ada Rehan," and she decided to stick with it. Her brother-in-law, Oliver Byron, got her a part in Across the Continent, giving her a good start in show business in 1873, when she was only thirteen years old. Ada eventually became one of America's greatest actresses, and as a member of Augustin Daly's company she excelled in classical comedy. Hattie Crehan married actor Sol Russell and they had a house on Columbia Avenue in North Long Branch.

Smiling and dancing a jig in the role of "Miss Jenny O'Jones," Ada Rehan's enthusiasm was captured by Sarony, c.1880s. Ada, a star member of Augustin Daly's stock company for many years, frequently visited her theatrical sisters Kate Byron and Hattie Russell at their North Long Branch homes. She owned a cottage there for only a very brief time before her death in 1916.

87 UNION SQR., N. Y.

The Perfect Vacation House

Oliver and Kate Byron first vacationed at the New Jersey shore in 1870. After the birth of their son, Arthur, on April 3, 1872, the Byrons decided to purchase a seashore home. They rented for a couple of seasons, then in 1875 they found a house that was just right. They purchased the cottage at 459 Ocean Avenue, North Long Branch, that had belonged to former New York congressman Churchill J. Cambreleng.

Real Estate Deals

With a keen eye for investment properties, Oliver Byron built or remodeled fourteen cottages in the North Long Branch and Monmouth Beach area during a twenty-three year period from 1882 to 1905. Byron managed to swing some good deals on land and constructed affordable cottages. The clever actor understood the importance of recycling materials. When Monmouth Park Racetrack was shut down due to the New Jersey ban on gambling in 1893, Byron purchased wood from the grandstand that was being demolished.[1]

CASTLE BYRON, OCEAN AVENUE, NORTH LONG BRANCH.

This pen and ink drawing of the "Castle Byron" at 459 Ocean Ave. in North Long Branch appeared in the *Long Branch Record*, 1902. The cottage that has since been replaced by a modern house was the summer home of the theatrical couple Oliver and Kate Byron and their son Arthur for many years. Byron built and acquired a number of cottages in the area as investment properties.

Also in 1893, he acquired stained glass windows from the cottage that once had been President Grant's Summer White House, when it was being remodeled, and used them in his construction projects.[2] Byron expanded his own Ocean Avenue house, adding six rooms to the existing twelve and moved the front porch to the rear, the ocean side of the cottage.

The Death of Garfield

Oliver and Kate Byron were well established in the Long Branch area when, in 1881, President Garfield was shot and badly wounded by a madman in Washington, D. C., on July 2nd. Garfield's wife, Lucretia, rushed from vacationing at Long Branch to be with her husband. Because of a malaria epidemic in the Potomac area, it was decided that Garfield should be brought to Long Branch to recover. With many offers of cottages, Mrs. Garfield chose the Francklyn Cottage by the sea owned by Charles Francklyn, head of the Cunard Line. In order to bring the ailing President directly to the Francklyn Cottage from the Elberon train station, local residents worked doggedly to lay a half mile of track in less than 24 hours, completing the spur in time for the President's arrival on September 6th. Reports were encouraging at first that President Garfield would recover, but he died at the Francklyn cottage on September 19th.

From Tracks to Teahouse

The makeshift train tracks were quickly dismantled, but the resourceful Oliver Byron had the foresight to preserve a piece of history. He purchased the railroad ties, had a small cabin built from them by a local carpenter named William Presley, and placed it on his property at "Castle Byron."

The simple little structure made from railroad ties has long been referred to as "Garfield's Hut" and was used as a teahouse by the Byron family. Resembling a child's log-cabin-style playhouse about 8 feet high, the structure consists of a single room, 8 feet x 12 feet with a Dutch door and windows with stained-glass borders on either side. Using a patriotic theme, Byron had the hut painted red, white, and blue.

"The Garfield Hut" on the grounds of The Church of the Presidents in Elberon, was restored in 2006. The small "tea house" that actor Oliver Byron had built was constructed with railroad ties from the temporary spur used to transport President Garfield after he was shot in 1881 to the Francklyn Cottage in Elberon.

Inside the hut, the actor and his wife entertained friends for tea, and allegedly Oliver would indulge in serving fine wines here.[3] Byron was said to store butter and cream for the tea parties in an icebox that was accessed by a trap door in the floor.[4]

Famous Guests

The Byrons' theatrical friends often visited them at North Long Branch. On July 14, 1889, *The New York Times* reported that Mrs. John Drew and her daughter, Mrs. Georgie Drew Barrymore, were staying at the Byron cottage on Ocean Avenue. A delightful account of their visit gives an idea of life during that era:

An engraving of men working through the night to lay the tracks for the wounded Garfield's train. Some of these railroad ties would be purchased by actor Oliver Byron to construct the now famous "hut."

"Little Marguerite Field, the child actress, is also with Mr. Byron. One day this week Mrs. Langtry (Lillie Langtry) went from Hattie Russell's cottage over to that of Mr. Byron. She was ill all the time she was here with throat trouble, and it was the first time Dr. Pemberton had permitted her to go out. She was sitting on the veranda. Little Marguerite was singing to herself in the parlor. Mr. Byron invited her to come outside and sing. She accepted the invitation. Mrs. Langtry's morning dress was caught up in front just sufficient to show her ankle. Little Marguerite went on singing. But suddenly she stopped, looked at Mrs. Langtry and exclaimed: 'Pull down your dress, sis; you're getting' (to be) a big girl now.' Mrs. Langtry shrieked with laughter; so did Mrs. Barrymore, Mrs. Drew, and Mr. Byron."

Sweet Charity

Oliver Doud Byron was always trying to give back to the community. In 1889 he directed "For Sweet Charity's Sake," a big benefit to raise money for the Monmouth Memorial Hospital in Long Branch (predecessor of today's Monmouth Medical Center). The show featured an incredible array of the top stars of the day, and most of them owned or rented summer homes in the area. Everyone chipped in to help: the Drews and Barrymores, Nellie McHenry, Neil Burgess, John Albaugh, and musical director Frank Maeder. The Messrs. Leland donated the use of the Ocean Theatre and orchestra. Local painters, florists, printers, and carpenters all offered their time and services without charge. It was one of the most glorious charity events ever held at the Jersey shore.

A Firehouse for North Long Branch

Oliver Byron, the once adored star of melodramas and "Summer Mayor" of North Long Branch, is almost forgotten today, but the local fire company he founded still bears his name. Always concerned about fire, Oliver Byron had a firehouse built in 1890 on Atlantic Avenue, near Ocean Avenue, and he donated the fire engine for the company that was called the Oliver Byron Hose Company No. 3 Still in operation, it is now the Oliver Byron Engine Company No. 5.

The Garfield Hut Preserved

Oliver Doud Byron fought against the powerful theatrical syndicate that took control of theatrical bookings in the late 19th and early 20th centuries, but did not win his battle. Byron died at his Ocean Avenue cottage on October 22, 1920, from a cerebral hemorrhage. Kate, his beloved wife of fifty years, died just two months later. Within a year, their son Arthur Byron sold the remaining four cottages in North Long Branch, including "Castle Byron." Arthur moved to the Highland Beach section of Sea Bright and took the Garfield Hut with him.

When he sold his property, Arthur gave the historic hut to its builder, William Garfield Presley. It then went to his son, Oliver Byron Presley, who lived on Atlantic Avenue and used the hut as a playhouse for his children. Presley eventually donated the hut to the Long Branch Historical Society and it was placed on the grounds of The Church of the Presidents (St. James Episcopal Chapel) on Ocean Avenue in Elberon.[5]

Arthur Byron's Success

Arthur Byron's name is perhaps recognized more often today than that of his father, because Arthur can be seen in old movies. Arthur got his start in one of his father's shows at a young age, then acted in numerous Broadway stage plays in the early twentieth century. He began a film career when he was middle aged and appeared in the classic 1934 horror film, *The Mummy*, with Boris Karloff. His wife, Kathryn (Keys) Byron, played the female lead in *The Mummy*. Arthur Byron was a founder of Actor's Equity and served as its president in the late 1930s. He died in 1943.

Oliver Byron Remembered

Oliver Doud and Mary Kate Byron made many worthwhile contributions to the communities of North Long Branch and Monmouth Beach. Kate was of great support to her husband and was helpful with the real estate deals. Byron's foresight in building homes at the Monmouth County shore and improving his community is admired. His salvaging railroad ties from the track built for President Garfield to create The Garfield Hut is one example of his enterprising accomplishments.

The Royal Family – The Barrymores

The names "Drew" and "Barrymore" have been revered by theater-goers for generations. Often referred to as "the royal family of the American theater," members of the Drew and Barrymore clans were among the theatrical families who summered at New Jersey shore resorts in the late 19th century. Although they did not own property there, the "royals" presence at hotels, friend's cottages, and rental homes always created a buzz.

Mum Mum's World

The colorful matriarch of the family, British-born Louisa Lane Drew (1820-1897), affectionately known as "Mum Mum," was a spunky actress who became director of the Arch Street Theater in Philadelphia.

Louisa Lane Drew, matriarch of the famous "Royal Family of the American Theater," is in costume as "Mrs. Malaprop," for this c.1890 portrait. She frequently visited the Monmouth County Shore with her three grandchildren who would become superstars of stage and screen - Lionel, Ethel, and John Barrymore.

She was widowed twice, then married comedian John Drew. After he died in 1862, she took over the management of the theater and ran it with "an iron hand" for thirty years.

Mrs. Drew's son, John Drew (1853-1927), followed in the family's footsteps as a renowned actor. Her daughter, Georgiana, known as "Georgie" (1856-1893), was an exceptionally beautiful comedienne. In 1875, Georgie married a dashing English actor named Herbert Blyth, who decided to go by the stage name Maurice Barrymore. "Barry," as he was called, turned out to be a heavy drinker with a fondness for women. All three of Georgie and Barry's children became celebrated stars of the stage and screen: Lionel (1878-1954), Ethel (1879-1959), and John (1882-1942).

The dashing Maurice Barrymore and his lovely wife Georgie Drew Barrymore, as seen in these two cabinet photos, were known to frequent Little Silver Point for their summer vacations in the 1880s. They were the parents of Lionel, Ethel, and John.

Georgie and Barry are said to have rented a house at Little Silver Point near Seven Bridge Road in the late 1880s. (In its early days, the now year-round residential town of Little Silver was frequented by summer sojourners.) After Georgie's untimely death at the age of thirty-seven from a lung ailment, Barry soon remarried, but lived a

A view of the Pontin House, opened in 1880, at Little Silver Point. The residential peninsula was once known for summer boarding houses that provided quiet retreats for actors and other famous visitors. *Dorn's Classic Images.*

roguish life and died in 1905 of complications from syphilis.

Sweet Charity

It was the dynamic Mum Mum who stepped in and cared for her three talented grandchildren when their mother died. The busy grandma found time to take her grandkids to the beaches of Monmouth and Ocean counties. She often visited theatrical friends at the New Jersey shore and stayed at "The Murray Cottage" on the North Long Branch oceanfront. At the cottage on the southwest corner of Atlantic and Ocean Avenues, she and her grandchildren enjoyed good times together by the sea.

Although they visited mainly to relax away from the theater, the family did donate their time to participate in charitable events now and then. A program from July 29, 1889, for a gala show to benefit the Monmouth Memorial Hospital at Long Branch, included recitations by Mrs. Drew. Georgie had appeared in a scene from *Othello* when her eleven-year-old son, Lionel Barrymore, was listed as a "programmer." (He passed out the programs!) Athough he became a famous actor, Lionel always insisted that he'd rather paint than act.

Mr. Barrymore's Etchings

Besides visiting North Long Branch and Little Silver, the Drews and the Barrymores spent time at the Curtis House, a popular hotel of the era at Point Pleasant Beach in Ocean County. They also stayed at the Davis family of literary fame's Point Pleasant summer home, "Vagabond's Rest."

In his later years despite physical problems, Lionel Barrymore, an accomplished artist, created some etchings of places with titles including "Point Pleasant" and "Old Red Bank" that were often reproduced. Although it was believed for many years that the etchings were of the New Jersey Shore, they may have represented places in other areas with the same or similar names. The exact locations remain a mystery, perhaps only the late artist could have verified the locales, or perhaps they were composites of places done from his memory.

Point Pleasant   Lionel Barrymore

This reproduction of an etching titled "Point Pleasant" by Lionel Barrymore, who spent youthful summers at the New Jersey Shore, was often reproduced commercially in the 1940s-1950s. For years, it was considered to be an Ocean County, New Jersey, scene but the location is not certain. It may have been created from memory and imagination by the actor, a prolific artist late in his life. Another etching by Barrymore, "Old Red Bank," is also questionable as to the location depicted. Reproductions of Barrymore's etchings, though charming and decorative, are abundant and inexpensive today.

Inexpensive but delightful reproductions of Lionel's etchings are often found in antique shops or flea markets as framed prints or on candy boxes. The original plates for the etchings are considered lost. The mass produced copies are of no significant monetary value but are fun to collect.

The Dynasty Continues

Although the "Royal Family" is long gone from the New Jersey shore, the Barrymore dynasty continues today with Drew Barrymore, granddaughter of the legendary John. Her great-grandmother, Mum Mum, would be so proud of her descendant, today's shining "royal" star.

A Thespian by the Sea – Louis James

From the wide verandah of his seaside cottage, Louis James enjoyed relaxing in a rocking chair and watching the waves whenever he could get away from the footlights. The distinguished classical stage actor built an oceanfront home at Monmouth Beach around the end of the nineteenth century.

Background

Born in Illinois in 1842, James joined a Louisville stock company at the age of twenty-one and earned only nine dollars a week. He left to work in Mrs. Drew's Philadelphia Arch Street Theatre and then became a member of Augustin Daly's New York Company. James was leading man in Lawrence Barrett's company until 1886 when he branched out on his own. Then, he produced and starred in a series of Shakespearean revivals that he had more success with on the road than in New York, though critics did have favorable praise for his work. Louis James married Shakespearean actress Marie Wainwright in 1879.

Louis James, a noted Shakespearean actor, had a home at Monmouth Beach. He was once a member of Mrs. John Drew's stock company in Philadelphia and he was Lawrence Barrett's leading man, before he branched out on his own in 1886. Here he appears on a "Between the Acts" little cigar card, part of a series of actors.

A Most Pleasant Interview

In 1902, a writer for *The Theatre* magazine interviewed James at the New Jersey Shore summer home and enjoyed sitting on the comfortable verandah while taking notes. He described the green lawn that stretched to the edge of the beach and the sound of the waves, "murmuring lazily and slowly the cadence of a summer sea." Mrs. James told the reporter how proud she was of the summer cottage that her husband had built and planned himself. Their son and daughter were away in the mountains at the time of the interview.

A postcard of the actor Louis James' cottage at Monmouth Beach, is postmarked 1908. An interesting feature of this colonial revival house is its intersecting gambrel-roofed gables.

As Falstaff, Louis James delighted the audience in Shakespeare's *The Merry Wives of Windsor* at the opening show of Frick's Lyceum on the river at Red Bank on September 4, 1906. Nellie McHenry of Highlands was popular in the role of Mistress Quickly.

Monkey Business

When the reporter entered the sumptuous James' cottage he was confronted with a trio of ceramic monkeys illustrating the old Japanese proverb, "We see no evil, we hear no evil, we speak no evil." One room in the actor's house was reserved for mementos of his roles including many photographs of himself in costume. In the late nineteenth century James and his wife, actress Marie Wainwright, appeared in plays together.

Louis James died in Montana while touring on March 6, 1910. According to his New York Times obituary, the star was "stricken with heart disease in his dressing room between the acts."

Louis James & his wife are relaxing on the wide verandah of their Monmouth Beach summer cottage. From *The Theatre*, September 1902, photo by Henry Block.

Two classical musicians of international fame who lived at Monmouth Beach. Violin virtuoso Albert Spalding (1888-1953) was born in Chicago where his father J.W. Spalding and uncle Albert Goodwill Spalding (a hall of fame baseball star who once had a mansion in Rumson) founded the Spalding sporting goods company. Born in Paris in 1880, Andre Benoist immigrated to the United States at a young age, became a leading accompanist and was invited to work with violinist Spalding. This photo is c.1920. *Courtesy of the Benoist family.*

Celebrated accompanist Andre Benoist rented this Shingle Style house (shown here c. 1915) at 24 Valentine St. in Monmouth Beach, that was built by actor Oliver Byron. In 1919, Benoist purchased a large, late Victorian house at 15 Valentine St. where he raised his family. *Courtesy of the Benoist family.*

Act III
Red Bank and Fair Haven

In the early 1800s, Red Bank on the North Shrewsbury River (known as the Navesink River) developed into a bustling port with steamboats hauling the Monmouth County farmers' produce to New York City. Merchants discovered Red Bank as an excellent center for stores that provided a place for the rural folk to visit the town for clothing, shoes, hardware, and perhaps take in a show.

Besides the steamboats, the railroad made the town comfortably close to New York City for theatrical people. Many of them owned summer places by the river in the late 1800s. By the close of the 1920s, the area was mostly home to year round residents.

Broad Street, Red Bank, today retains many of its early buildings that are seen in this early twentieth century photograph, looking south from Front St.. During the first three decades of the twentieth century, there were at least five vaudeville/movie theaters in the busy town where country folk would come for shopping and entertainment.

Early Theaters of Red Bank

The Opera House

Prior to 1883, theatrical entertainment in Red Bank was held at the Music Hall in the Adlem & Cole dry goods store building at 30 Broad St., now Jack's Music Shoppe, and at other commercial buildings, halls and lodges. The first *real* theater in Red Bank was The Red Bank Opera House located on the south side of West Front St. near Maple Ave. Built by Charles G. Allen, it opened on October 29, 1883 with a stunning performance by Rose Eytinge, "a celebrated emotional actress." The facility featured not only plays and light operas, but boxing tournaments as well. The 1890s saw great interest in "sparring matches" and the entire theater including the gallery would be filled to capacity for the popular athletic events. The Red Bank Chief of Police would attend to be sure the boxers fought fairly and no doubt to keep the enthusiastic crowd under control.

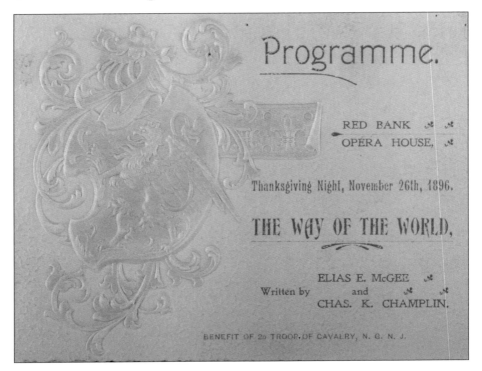

An original 1896 program for a benefit performance of *The Way of the World* at the Red Bank Opera House features local business owners in the cast. The play, written by professional Red Bank area stars Charles Champlin and Elias McGee, featured photographer J.W. Foxwell, architect Leon Cubberly, and cigar store owner, Mortimer Pach.

The Final Performances

Until 1905, The Red Bank Opera House continued to be a popular venue that stayed open during the summer to attract the vacationing crowd from Red Bank and neighboring towns. On Wednesday, June 21, 1905, vaudevillians who summered at Fair Haven put on a benefit for the Fair Haven fire company at the Red Bank Opera House under the direction of Frank Martineau, a theatrical manager who lived in Fair Haven. The evening that featured a hilarious parody of the popular drama *Way Down East* proved to be a great success.

The show booked for the next three nights, June 22-24, was the "Boston Ideal Opera Co." The troupe that specialized in light opera called opera bouffe was scheduled to appear in Asbury Park the following week. The well-publicized company of some forty performers, who brought along elaborate costumes and scenery, stayed at the Central Hotel (formerly French's Central Hotel on the corner of W. Front St. and Maple Ave. The building was torn down in 1995) conveniently right next to the theater. Although summer was just beginning, the weather was hot and the theater's manager J.W. Eyles reportedly went to New York to purchase some fans earlier that week. Ads for the shows stated "House will be cooled with Electric Fans," quite a treat for the audiences of that era.

This well dressed troupe of famous little people appeared at the Red Bank Opera House in 1898 according to the back of this cabinet photo. Their names are signed on the reverse as follows: "Mrs. Thos. Thumb, Count Magri her husband, Baron Magri, Annie Nelson, Gen. Liable."

A Raging Fire

After The Boston Ideal Opera Company completed two success-ful nights, at around three a.m. on Saturday morning, a terrible fire broke out in the Opera House. A night watchman at nearby Mount's Carriage Factory turned in the alarm and the Red Bank Volunteer Fire Company responded promptly. However, the blaze was already raging out of control and the roof caved in. The firemen did their best to save the neighboring buildings, including The Central Hotel. The opera cast and crew were awakened and by the fire alarm. *The Red Bank Register* described the mayhem that followed:

> "Some of the actresses grabbed up their clothing, ran downstairs and ran outside scantily clad. As soon as they saw they would have time to pack their trunks, even if the hotel should catch on fire, they hastened back to their rooms and filled their trunks with their personal property. The trunks were then brought down stairs by the firemen and others and deposited on the walk on the other side of the street."

None of the actors were hurt but several firemen suffered minor injuries. Sheet musical scores, librettos, props, and scenery were destroyed in the blaze. The opera company did not have insurance, as the premiums were so outrageously high for traveling theatrical companies. Their losses were around $10,000, a large amount back then. The performer's personal collections of music were irreplace-able. The cause of the fire was never determined and the theater was not rebuilt.

Frick's Lyceum by the River

Fred Frick, a well-known theater manager and an accomplished bicyclist built a new theater in 1906 called The Lyceum on the edge of the Navesink River where a canning factory once stood. The site was at today's Marine Park, adjacent to the historic Red Bank Boat Club, in the area where tennis courts are located. Frick's theater designed by architect William A. Shoemaker had a seating capacity of 1,416. The floor was of white maple and the curved backed seats were of bird's-eye maple with a natural finish. The stage, forty feet deep and fifty feet wide was as large as the regulation stages in New York theaters. The fifty-five foot high stage accommodated scenery that could be hoisted up and out of sight, unlike many earlier theaters that simply pushed it back. The décor featured elegant white and gold and dazzling electric lighting was everywhere. Just a few days before opening night, carpenters and craftsmen were working extra hours to complete the state of the art auditorium. The place had no basement, a safety feature as many theater fires originated in basements.

Red Bank theatrical manager and entrepreneur Fred Frick poses on his "big wheel" bike while Charles Noble holds him steady, c.1895. Frick obviously liked to show off his medals won in cycling competitions.
Dorn's Classic Images

Not everything was complete for the opening night, but Frick felt it was good enough to open and all the work was finished soon thereafter. It was a gala debut in Red Bank on Labor Day, September 3, 1906. Extra trolleys were even added to accommodate the theater-goers. The performance was Shakespeare's jovial *The Merry Wives of Windsor*. Louis James (of Monmouth Beach) starred as Falstaff and Nellie McHenry (of Highlands) played Mistress Quickly. The following month, the show with sets and all, went to New York City's Amsterdam Theater with the same stars in the leading roles. The next performance at Frick's enormously popular Lyceum was George M. Cohan's New York musical comedy success, *Forty-five Minutes From Broadway*. When it opened on September 13, the Lyceum was complete. The theater by the riverside continued to present popular shows such as *High-Class Vaudeville* and plays directly from New York including the wildly popular play *Buster Brown*.

To celebrate the grand opening of Fred Frick's New Lyceum Theatre in August 1906, a flotilla of boats assembled on the North Shrewsbury River (Navesink River). In the area of today's Marine Park, the large theater (now the site of tennis courts) can be seen to the left of the historic Red Bank Boat Club building that still stands.

Dancing at the Lyceum

On June 2, 1915, the Lyceum re-opened under new management and it was quite a different place. The opening performance was a concert by a Hungarian orchestra with dancing exhibitions. Patrons were served refreshments including ice cream, grape juice, and soda by "girl waiters" right at their seats. By October, 1915, the Lyceum was being used as a dancing pavilion where spectators were able to watch the dancers from the gallery. It cost five cents a dance or six dances for a quarter and frankfurters and soft drinks could be purchased.

The new Lyceum was a far different place from the original theater where Louis James delighted the audience as Falstaff. But now the Great War was going on in Europe, soldiers were stationed at nearby Fort Vail (Fort Monmouth) preparing for whatever might happen, and the silent movies were becoming wildly popular.

Matinees and Evenings

Several theaters for vaudeville and movies opened in Red Bank between 1910 and 1930. The Bijou, a small moving picture house that was on Monmouth Street across from the railroad station, had a seating capacity of 364. In 1911, the *Red Bank Register* states that "Red Bank has a moving picture theater that ranks among the best." In 1914, ads appeared for The Majestic Theater, a motion picture house "Opposite Depot – Monmouth St." that was under "under new management. (Apparently, The Bijou became The Majestic). They ran promotions such as drawings for a half ton of coal and "Mother's Home-made Pie Night."

"Mr. Barnum of Red Bank" was the name his New York associates dubbed Mr. M.E. Mc-Nulty, but the locals simply addressed him as "Mr. Mack." McNulty managed The Empire and The Palace theaters in Red Bank during the early years of the twentieth century.
Red Bank Public Library

The Empire Theater was a small, well-attended vaudeville house on Monmouth Street, closer to Broad St., managed by local showman M.E. McNulty who was dubbed "Mr. Barnum of Red Bank." The Empire featured animal acts, dancers, magicians, comedy teams, and a variety of unusual acts. Their ads promised, "Another Sparkling Show, The Magnet That Draws the Crowds."

The Lyric Theater, which ran along Wharf Ave., was built in 1912 by the Red Bank Amusement Co., and had its entrance on E. Front Street across from the Globe Hotel. A long and narrow lobby led back to the large theater that was designed for both live shows and moving pictures. For a very short period of time in 1919 the Lyric was known as Ferber's Theater and then it became The Palace in 1920. It was leased by none other than "Mr. Barnum of Red Bank" after the Empire Theater shut down.

The Empire's roof had collapsed that January, 1920. The vaudeville theater on Monmouth Street was ruined when the roof caved in from heavy snow accumulations.

A 1913 ad for Red Bank's Empire Theater that was on Monmouth Street gives an idea of the type of entertainment that was popular at the time.

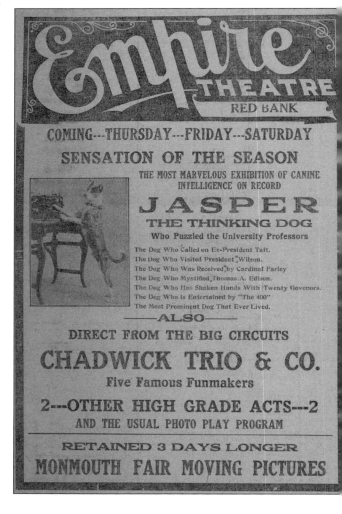

Empire THEATRE
RED BANK

COMING---THURSDAY---FRIDAY---SATURDAY

SENSATION OF THE SEASON

THE MOST MARVELOUS EXHIBITION OF CANINE INTELLIGENCE ON RECORD

JASPER

THE THINKING DOG

Who Puzzled the University Professors

The Dog Who Called on Ex-President Taft.
The Dog Who Visited President Wilson.
The Dog Who Was Received by Cardinal Farley
The Dog Who Mystified Thomas A. Edison.
The Dog Who Has Shaken Hands With Twenty Governors.
The Dog Who Is Entertained by "The 400"
The Most Prominent Dog That Ever Lived.

---ALSO---

DIRECT FROM THE BIG CIRCUITS

CHADWICK TRIO & CO.

Five Famous Funmakers

2---OTHER HIGH GRADE ACTS---2

AND THE USUAL PHOTO PLAY PROGRAM

RETAINED 3 DAYS LONGER

MONMOUTH FAIR MOVING PICTURES

Fortunately, a tragedy was averted as no one was inside at the time but a half hour later, it would have been full of patrons.

The Palace was purchased at a sheriff's sale in 1928 and operated by performer and theatrical manager Tony Hunting, a Fair Haven resident. This was a wise move on Hunting's part as the "talkies" were beginning and business was booming.

The Strand Theater in Red Bank first opened in 1917 with a Mary Pickford movie, *Poor Little Rich Girl*. Its first projectionist was Daniel D. Dorn, inventor and film maker, who started a photography business on Wallace St. in 1936 with his son, Daniel W. Dorn. Located on the northeast corner of Broad St. and Borden St. (now Linden Place), The Strand remained open until the 1950s when it became a Lerner's Shop and in 1991, the present offices of Merrill Lynch were constructed on the site. Remnants of the old theater including decorative 1920s theatrical wall murals were revealed but determined not feasible to save.

Pictured here in the 1922, Red Bank's Strand Theater on Broad Street, a popular vaudeville and movie house, first opened in 1917. It was replaced by a clothing shop in the 1950s and is now the site of a brokerage. *Dorn's Classic Images.*

Red Bank's grandest theater, The Carlton, located on Monmouth St. opened with a gala affair on November 11, 1926 with many well known theatrical and political guests attending. The opening show was Keith Albee vaudeville along with a feature film, *The Quarterback* with Richard Dix. The two theaters in Red Bank that stayed open for the longest periods of time were The Carlton and The Strand that both belonged to the Reade movie chain for many years. The only survivor of the old Red Bank theaters today is the former Carlton, now The Count Basie Theater, which has recently undergone extensive restoration.

Red Bank's Comical Couple —
Mestayer and Vaughn

A long forgotten but intriguing theatrical couple who lived in Red Bank during the 1880s and 1890s was William A. Mestayer and Theresa Vaughn. Their hilarious stage plays had American audiences rolling in the aisles as the Mestayer troupe toured the country. One of their biggest hits of the early 1880s, *Tourists* was so recognized that it was often advertised only by its subtitle, *A.P.P.C.* (A Pullman Palace Car). Mestayer and Vaughn acted in the popular comedy and Mestayer designed the innovative scenery. The actor patented his blueprints for a set that simulated the interior of a sleeping car with backdrops of trees and mountains outside the windows, providing a realistic look that the pre-movie era audiences found impressive.

Starting Young

Born William Ayres Haupt in Philadelphia in 1846, Mestayer made his stage debut at the tender age of eight, and then worked in stock companies including the California Theater in San Francisco before forming his own troupe. His first wife divorced him.

Theresa Vaughn, Mestayer's adored second wife, was an exceptionally beautiful young performer with "come hither" eyes, a lovely voice, and a flair for comedy. Theresa was a member of the well-known theatrical family named Ott. Born in New York City but sent to Boston to study at a convent, she was the oldest of thirteen children and trained her younger siblings for theatrical careers. When she married William Mestayer, Theresa was only fifteen years old and at sixteen she acted with her husband in *Tourists*. Her biggest hit was *We, Us & Co.*, another Mestayer comedy.

The Gift of Laughter

William and Theresa owned a riverside house on Rector Place where they summered for years and became well known around Red Bank. Their property can be seen on a late nineteenth century map of Red Bank in the name of "Theresa Haupt." At the big 1889 benefit for the Monmouth Memorial Hospital at Long Branch, Theresa sang a popular song and her husband performed in a tongue-in-cheek op-

eretta, "The Jersey Nightigale," a spoof of the great opera star Adelina Patti, that was the side-splitting finale of the hospital show.

In the early 1880s, theatrical photographer Napoleon Sarony captured the coquettish beauty of Theresa Vaughn, the young wife and comedic partner of William Mestayer. In their day, they were well known residents of Red Bank.

37 UNION SQR., N. Y.

Two delightful advertising cards for William Mestayer's comedy about railroad travel. In the late nineteenth century, Mestayer and his wife Theresa Vaughn maintained
a home in Red Bank but toured the country by rail with their play about tourists
journeying across America on a Pullman car!

William Mestayer died from a kidney disease in 1896 at the age
of fifty. After his death, and the death of one of her brothers who
was an actor also living in Red Bank, Theresa suffered from mental
health problems. In 1901, she was committed to "an insane asylum"
in Worchester, Massachusetts. The once sparkling comedy star died at
the institution while still only in her thirties, on October 7, 1903.

Though sadly forgotten today, Mestayer and Vaughn brought
laughter and joy to early theatrical stages.

The Kid from Red Bank –
William "Count" Basie

"Another thing I like to remember about Red Bank back when I was a
boy was the way things used to be during the Christmas season. Sometimes

I see something that makes me remember how the streets used to look when all the pines and fir trees and all the decorations were up, and all the Christmas merchandise was displayed out on the sidewalks."[1]

—William "Count" Basie

The Early Years of a Jazz Legend

The tale of Red Bank's theatrical past cannot be complete without the story of a native son who became a star, William "Count" Basie. The legendary jazz pianist, composer, and bandleader of the swing era was born August 21, 1904, in Red Bank. His parents, Harvey Lee Basie and Lillian Ann Childs Basie, were both musically inclined. "The Kid from Red Bank" (the name of one of his hit recordings) had one older brother named Leroy. The Basie family owned a modest house at 229 Mechanic Street.[2]

Harvey Basie, Count William Basie's father, poses, c. 1972, with the piano that his son first learned to play on some sixty years earlier. The Basie house on Mechanic Street was undergoing reconstruction. Well-known Red Bank artist Evelyn Leavens happened to be riding by, saw Mr. Basie leaning against the piano, stopped, hopped out, and cried, "Please, don't move!" She got her camera out of the car and captured the scene. *Dorn's Classic Images.*

Harvey Basie worked at the riverfront home of Judge White as a coachman. When automobiles took over for horses, Harvey continued as a groundskeeper for the White family and other well-to-do homeowners at their sprawling estates in the area. Lillian, who earned money for her family by taking in laundry and baking from home, encouraged her son William to play the piano. Lillian taught him herself at first but then bought him lessons with a local German woman and made sure he practiced. Bill did the exercises but he didn't need to look at notes. He was so adept that he could simply play almost anything he heard.

Wanderlust

Young Bill Basie liked the piano, but the drums were his favorite instrument at first. His Dad even bought him a trap drum. A typical youth, Bill or Willie as he was sometimes called, enjoyed hanging out with friends by the dock on the river and having a good time. But Basie wasn't idle; he helped his Dad with jobs at the estates, and he worked as a carrier for the Red Bank newspaper, *The Daily Register.* He attended Red Bank public schools but quit after junior high school. He eventually said, "I should have gone on and finished school, but I just wanted to hurry up and get out of there and out of Red Bank and be going somewhere." Whenever a carnival would come to Red Bank, young Basie would chat with the itinerant performers and wish he could join them.

Accompanying the Silent Movies

Bill Basie managed to find his way into the Red Bank theaters where he would observe vaudeville acts, fill in as a projectionist and do miscellaneous odd jobs. At that time, some theaters were still segregated with separate seating areas for blacks. The Lyric Theater on East Front Street was one of the places where young Basie learned about show business. (The Lyric became The Palace but Basie refers to them as two different theaters.) He would later attribute his affinity for the organ to those early days when he frequented a Red Bank theater to hear Harold LaRoss play the organ for the silent movies.[3] Basie said:

"I guess show business got into my system early. By all odds, my favorite place in Red Bank was the Palace moving picture theater. I used to go down there and do chores for the manager every chance I got. I would help sweep out the auditorium and the lobby, polish the brass rails and fixtures and put up the extra seats."[4]

Basie would also go to the railroad station to meet performers when they came in and he'd show them the way to the theaters. One day, the regular accompanist at one of the theaters, who commuted from New York, did not show up and Basie was asked to fill in for him. Basie knew what to do as he had observed it all so many times. He simply looked at the screen and improvised the appropriate type of music for a melodrama, or a western, or a comedy.

Out into the World

Bill Basie met up with percussionist Sonny Greer from Long Branch, who later played with the great Duke Ellington. Feeling that he couldn't compete with Greer on the drums, Basie chose to stick with the piano. Basie and a friend from Eatontown decided to leave school and go out into the world as musicians. As the roaring '20s and prohibition began, they played in clubs in Asbury Park and at a roadhouse, The Hong Kong Inn.

In 1924, Basie moved to New York City's Harlem, the paradise for the hottest music of the era. At the height of the Harlem renaissance, he learned his craft from celebrated jazz musicians and the stride pianists including Fats Waller. Basie then got booked on a vaudeville circuit that took him to many cities.

Going to Kansas City

As luck would have it, Basie became stranded in a place that turned out to be of great importance in his life - Kansas City. It was a hotbed of jazz! Basie played with Walter Page's Blue Devils in 1928 and by the following year he had hooked up with the up-coming Bennie Moten's band as a pianist and assistant conductor. Moten's group was headed towards nationwide fame when things took an unexpected turn in 1935. After Moten's death at forty-one from complications of a routine tonsillectomy, Basie started a new band called Count Basie and the Barons of Rhythm. It was the start of his illustrious career as the "Count." Dance bands were sizzling and the swing era was going into full swing! By the close of 1936,

Basie had signed a contract with Decca Records and started recording. During this period, the band recorded such great hits as "One O'Clock Jump," "Jumping at the Woodside" and "Taxi War Dance."

William "Count" Basie appears on this souvenir postcard, "A Mutsoscope Card." from the late 1930s. A series of these cards depicting various bandleaders and musicians of the 1930s-1940s were produced during that era and are affordable and popular collectibles today. Although associated with Kansas City, Basie was born and raised in Red Bank.

A Night to Remember

At the age of thirty-three, Red Bank's now-famous, native son returned for a first hometown appearance with his band. Although they had played Asbury Park the previous year, it was the band's first time in Red Bank. The one-night performance, a benefit for the Westside branch of the YMCA was held at the River Street School on February 3, 1938.[5] Dr. James W. Parker Sr., Red Bank's well-respected African American physician, contributed much to the community and was a leader of the YMCA. Through Dr. Parker's efforts, the concert was made possible. More than 500 people attended the rousing show. The audience didn't even feel the cold on that winter night as they were swinging and swaying to the sounds of Basie and his band. The program also featured the young blues singer Billie Holiday and the great James Rushing who delighted the crowd as he sang "Rosalie." Holiday, known as "Lady Day," would leave Basie's troupe the following month to work with the Artie Shaw Orchestra, an all-white band. On Easter Sunday, 1938, she appeared with Shaw at the Casino in Asbury Park.

The February 3, 1938, benefit concert at Red Bank represents a memorable event during the waning Depression years when "The Kid from Red Bank" brought joy to the people of his hometown. It is significant not only as a piece of jazz history that benefited a good cause, but also because it brought together a racially mixed audience. The music attracted a diverse crowd of local people together that night during a time when both formal and informal segregation still prevailed. And yet improvements had been made since Basie's childhood at Red Bank, and the times were changing...or at least it was a beginning.

Passages

In 1942, Basie married Catherine Morgan, a gorgeous dancer who was on the vaudeville circuits. Their daughter, Diane, was born in 1944. After World War II, and as the 1940s came to a close, the big bands declined in popularity. Basie returned to New York City where the Count Basie Orchestra stayed until Basie disbanded the group in 1950. The band was re-established two years later and embarked on highly successful world tours. Even as rock-and-roll hit the charts,

Basie recorded a hit single in 1955 with blues singer Joe Williams. The Count kept "a high profile," making recordings with top stars, including Ella Fitzgerald, Tony Bennett, Sarah Vaughn, and Frank Sinatra. Basie remained popular and toured the word during the 1960s and early 1970s. But in 1976, The Count had to slow down after suffering a heart attack, and he moved his family to the Bahamas. Basie's beloved wife of over forty years, "Katy," died in 1983 and "The Kid from Red Bank" performed in his hometown for a benefit at the Carlton in April of 1983. A year later, April 1984, Count William Basie died of cancer at the age of seventy-nine.

In Honor of The Count

Flags in Monmouth County were flown at half mast in honor of "The Kid from Red Bank" who gained worldwide fame. Not long after Basie's death in 1984, the historic Carlton Theater on Monmouth Street changed its name to "The Count Basie Theater." In 2004, Red Bank celebrated the one-hundredth anniversary of Basie's birth.

Opened in 1926, The Carlton Theater on Red Bank's Monmouth Street was designed by well-known Newark theater architect William E. Lehman. The Carlton featured live acts, concerts, and films. This photo is from 1950. The theater's name was changed to The Count Basie Theater in 1984, the year of the legendary musician's death. It has undergone extensive restoration and thrives today offering a wide array of live shows and concerts. *Dorn's Classic Images.*

Fair Haven's Bohemians – The Vaudevillians

True to its name, the pretty and tranquil village of Fair Haven (to the east and adjacent to Red Bank) was home to less than a thousand people in the 1890s. Fishermen, oystermen, farmers, carpenters, and laborers who worked on neighboring estates comprised the majority of full time residents. The town had a free black community since before the Civil War. In the late nineteenth and early twentieth century, steamboats on the New York-Red Bank route such as The Sea Bird and The Albertina made stops at Fair Haven bringing visitors including theatrical people eager to escape from the heat and stress of city life. Eventually, the influx of summer visitors declined and Fair Haven became a year round residential community.

An Unpretentious Paradise

In the 1890s, players from the vaudeville circuits found Fair Haven to be an ideal and affordable summer retreat that tolerated their bohemian ways. At first, the weary performers stayed at boarding houses and hotels in town - The Atlantic Hotel, The Van Tine, The Pine View and others - to get some rest before the theatrical season would start up again in September and they would "trod the boards" again.

This c.1910 scene, depicted on a postcard, is looking west from the east end of Fair Haven's River Road (near Doughty Lane) in the general area of the late nineteenth to early twentieth century vaudevillians' colony.

Henry C. Miner, a New York theater owner and a pioneer of vaudeville, was one of the first performers to settle at Fair Haven in the early 1890s. He had a large home on the river called "The Grange" for which Grange Ave. is named.

Ralph Smith, who went by the stage name George S. Lockwood, another performer associated with Fair Haven, lived on Kemp Ave. and worked as a motorman on the trolley that ran between Red Bank, Fair Haven and Rumson. Smith came to the town for a weekend after serving in the Spanish American War and ended up staying for fifty years. Smith and two of his theatrical friends secured positions on the Fair Haven police force "because they had the necessary uniforms in their costume trunks."[1]

On July 15, 1914, the *Red Bank Register* reported that about 175 actors were at Fair Haven for the summer. "The effect of this influx of actors always shows itself in livelier times and greater festivity at Fair Haven." The article mentions a lawn party to be held under a big tent, and a planned outing to Sandy Hook. The activities at the houseboat of the Players' boat club were in full swing and some actors even rehearsed there for the coming season. Many of the vaudevillians owned motorboats. One boat, *The Tango Kid* had recently broken loose from its moorings and drifted ashore. While it was marooned on the beach, someone stole a ham and eighteen eggs from the boat's pantry!

Scandals of Fair Haven

Many of the theatrical crowd who summered at Fair Haven were couples, some with children, simply looking for a safe and quiet place to spend their family vacations after stressful tours on the Vaudeville circuits. There were renters, but many of them decided to purchase homes. Some of them planned to spend their retirement years in Fair Haven. The offbeat performers did not feel restrained and thought nothing of walking down to the river from their cottages in bathing costumes, a pretty risqué act in the eyes of older residents with traditional Victorian ideas. But in Fair Haven, the actors seemed to be accepted whereas such behavior was not allowed at the oceanfront resorts.

One scandalous incident that did shock Fair Haven concerned local theatrical personality Elias Magee who, with Charles K. Champlin, produced shows at the Red Bank Opera House. In 1900, Magee "ran off with a dancer from one of the troupes, leaving his wife and two small daughters in poverty."[2] But, for the most part, the singers, dancers, tightrope walkers, whistlers, acrobats, magicians, jugglers, trained dogs, and a few exotic beasts became accepted as friendly, likeable citizens of Fair Haven. Their comfy abodes were mostly on the east side of town, near the Rumson border, an area that became known as "the actors' colony."

Perhaps one of the most unusual performers in the area was Hap Handy. The affable man who lived on Willow St. was a "bubbler." He delighted audiences by demonstrating his skill at manipulating soap bubbles, even putting colors inside of them and creating exquisite designs.

Forever Blowing Bubbles. Vaudevillian Hap Handy distinguished himself as a professional "bubbler." He manipulated soap bubbles! He poses here with a child's goat cart in front of his home on Willow St. in Fair Haven. *Courtesy of Marilyn Ambrosio.*

The "Hart" of Fair Haven

Harry Blocksom and Annie Hart were a well-known theatrical couple who had a home at 918 River Road. According to McMahon, Annie Hart convinced her husband Harry that they should live in Fair Haven in 1898. Blocksom worked with another male comedian named Burns in an act appropriately called "Blocksom & Burns." Annie Hart, born in Lawrence, Massachusetts, c. 1860, first appeared onstage in *The Black Crook* at Niblo's Garden in New York and then became a great star of Tony Pastor's music hall. She also toured all over the United States and Great Britain. The popular singer's biggest hit song was "The Hat Me Father Wore."

Annie enjoyed good times during her summers at Fair Haven and even served as a mascot and cheerleader for the local semi-pro baseball team, "The Foxes."

Annie Hart was even given the honorary title of "Sheriff of Fair Haven" – that's how well liked and respected she was in the town! She and Blocksom divorced but Annie stayed in Fair Haven. Annie owned several homes over the years at Fair Haven. She spent most of her life in the theater and appeared in the 1928 production of Jerome Kern's *Show Boat*.

An early image of Fair Haven vaudevillian Annie Hart in a military style costume and wearing tights (quite risqué for the Victorian era!). This tiny "Tiger Cheroot Cigarettes" card, c.1880s had to be a delightful prize for the purchaser.

After her retirement from the theater, she lived with Mr. and Mrs. Howard Marsh at their home in Rumson. Marsh, who started as an Irish tenor in vaudeville, was in *Show Boat* at the same time as Annie Hart, in 1928. In his later years, he ran a nightclub in northern New Jersey. Annie Hart died in 1947 in Fair Haven.

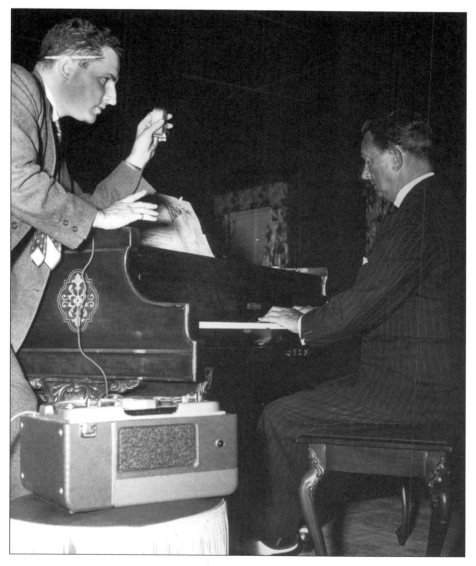

Monmouth County author and historian George H. Moss Jr. is pictured making a tape recording of vaudeville singer Howard Marsh in 1951. A Rumson resident for many years, Marsh was in the 1928 Broadway cast of *Show Boat. Moss Archives.*

A Theatrical Mayor

The old expression "born in a trunk" could be used to describe Tony Hunting's origins. His father ran a circus called "Bob Hunting's Circus" where Tony, who was born in 1890, learned the essentials of show business at an early age. In 1898, the Hunting show set up their tent on a then vacant lot on Wharf Ave. in Red Bank. Tony worked as an acrobat and horseback rider, but then gravitated towards vaudeville as he grew up. He and his wife, Corinne Frances, performed their variety act all over the United States. During the First World War, they traveled to France to entertain the troops, and when the war ended,

Looking at this c. 1905 postcard of Tony Hunting when he was a young performer, it's hard to believe he would eventually serve as a mayor of Fair Haven! The vaudevillian and Red Bank theater manager and his wife Corinne were well respected local citizens.

Hunting was named entertainment director for the army of occupation in Germany. Tony and his wife Corrine lived in a house on the corner of River Road and Doughty Lane. He managed several theaters in Monmouth County over the years. Tony Hunting died in February 1974.

The Players Boat Club

The members of the Fair Haven actors' colony blended in nicely with their neighbors at the village of Fair Haven by 1910. The vaudevillians kept their houses tidy and they helped with community services. But, they needed a place to socialize, a place to call their own after a tough season of "playing the boards." The actors of Fair Haven, held a meeting at the home of Tony and Corinne Hunting. The group agreed that it would be a great idea to buy a houseboat to use as their club's quarters. A houseboat that would fit the bill was available in Red Bank but the actors' group didn't have enough cash in their treasury to purchase it. The clever troupers came up with a logical fund raising solution – they would put on a show to raise the money!

The vaudevillians paraded down the street in Red Bank in an open car motorcade ending at Frick's Lyceum where their show was presented. It was an extravaganza that gave the group the $250 needed to buy the houseboat and have it towed to Fair Haven where they docked it at the end of Brown's Lane.

The Players Club officially opened on July 4, 1910, and Tom Morrissey was elected the first President and Tony Hunting was Vice-President. The benefit show became a tradition that was held annually at various theaters in Red Bank for over thirteen years.

A Bigger and Better Club

The houseboat rocked with fun and laughter as the performers enjoyed parties and dances at their river site. Besides the resident thespians, great stars including Al Jolson and Eddie Cantor were reputed to be guests at the club. The place became so popular, that it soon became clear that a larger facility would be needed. In July 1915, the players put on a benefit performance at Red Bank's Empire Theater. The show featured musicians, singers, and a comedy sketch by Charley Grapewin and his wife Anna Chance. (Grapewin is best remembered today for his role as "Uncle Henry" in the 1939 film version of *The Wizard of Oz* with Judy Garland. He and Chance had a summer home on Bath Ave. in Long Branch.)

The Players' Boat Club at Fair Haven, a lively association for theater folk only, began with a small houseboat in 1910, was replaced by a larger one in 1915, and then by a stationary structure in 1929. This is a photo of the second one. *Dorn's Classic Images.*

The well-attended event realized $1,200 that would be used toward buying a new boathouse. After the performance, the players and their friends went to Fair Haven on a special trolley, just for them, to a lawn party held on the grounds of a hotel.

A second houseboat was purchased for $2,500 and towed from New York to Fair Haven. It rested for its first winter in Fourth Creek (off Battin Rd. – the creek was much deeper and wider then) and was moved to the river in the spring. Improvements were made including adding a kitchen and a balcony. The original houseboat was converted to a bungalow and moved to Elm St.[3]

A Permanent "Houseboat"

In the Fall of 1928, a bad storm tore the houseboat from its moorings and washed it ashore, causing serious damage. Thirty-five members of the club met at the Hunting Theater (the former Palace) and pledged $3,000 towards the cost of a new clubhouse. They agreed that it would be too difficult to repair the old houseboat, so they decided to build a new stationary clubhouse. The proposed two-story structure that would cost $12,000 was to be built on pilings and to give the look and feel of a boat with wide decks around the building and nautical decorations. On July 10, 1929, the new Players' Boat Club building officially opened with a dance and cabaret that lasted till four in the morning.

A jovial group of theatrical people pose for a portrait during one of their costume or "old clothes" parties at The Players' Boat Club in Fair Haven, c.1930. No longer for players only, the updated and active boating club today is known as The Shrewsbury River Yacht Club. Photo by Louis Mendel, Red Bank.

Everything Changes

By the 1930s, movies were exceeding vaudeville and live theater in popularity and radio had entered American homes. Many of the older performers who made their living doing live performances had passed on. The actors' colony homes were updated and purchased by new residents, younger families who would come to live in the town and enjoy the lures of the river. The membership of the Players' Boat Club was no longer limited to theatrical folk as yachtsmen and sailing enthusiasts from all walks of life embraced the club. It became a true boating club rather than a theatrical alliance but its razzle-dazzle history was never forgotten. The place went through frequent remodeling and survived devastating storms over the years, but thrives today as the Shrewsbury River Yacht Club.

"The Irish Queen" - Maggie Cline

One of the Red Bank and Fair Haven area's most celebrated residents, the lusty red-headed Maggie Cline, would clench her fists, then swing her arms and hips as if shadow boxing while she sang "Throw Him Down McClosky." The ballad about an interracial boxing match never failed to rouse her audiences. Maggie often said the only man she ever met who didn't like the song was her father who chided her by saying, "Maggie, it ain't lady like."

"The Bowery Brunnhilde" (one of Maggie's nicknames), was born to Irish immigrant parents on January 1, 1857, in Haverhill Massachusetts. (Some sources say she was born in Maine.) When Maggie was only twelve years old, she went to work at a shoe factory where she entertained her co-workers by singing. Within a few years she decided she

The feisty Irish vaudeville star Maggie Cline puts up her dukes as she belts out "Throw Him Down McClosky," her signature song. Maggie resided in Fair Haven. *Courtesy of Carol A. Snapp.*

wanted to be in the theater and landed a job with a stage company in Boston for three dollars a week plus board. When the troupe left Boston to tour the west, Maggie's untrained but strong voice and personality made a big hit with the miners and ranchers who called her "The Irish Queen," a title that would stick with her.

Mrs. Ryan of Red Bank

Maggie returned to the East and after a bit of hard luck, got her career back on track and achieved great success on the vaudeville circuits. She married a café proprietor, not in the limelight, named John Ryan in 1888. Mr. and Mrs. Ryan lived in Red Bank in the former Enoch Cowart house at the corner of Broad Street and Irving Place. The couple later moved to the former Hendrickson house at the corner of Spring and East Front Streets. Maggie Cline Ryan made the following comment about Red Bank: "It is quiet and respectable and, so long as you keep square with the butcher and the rest of them, you're a leading citizen."

At Philadelphia in 1890, Maggie met John W. Kelly, "the rolling mill man" and purchased a song from him. She wanted to knock the price down even more, but ended up paying two dollars for "Throw Him Down McClosky." It proved to be her most memorable piece, partly because of the gestures and acting she added to her performance. She knew how to involve the audience who would cheer and join in on the chorus. Her repertoire included other popular numbers including "Nothing's Too Good for the Irish," "Slide, Kelly, Slide" and "Down Went McGinty to the Bottom of the Sea."

Retirement

Maggie retired in 1919 after forty-six years on the stage. She and her husband moved to Hance Road in Fair Haven, where Maggie Cline Ryan died on June 11, 1934, at the age of seventy-seven, outliving many of her colleagues. She was buried in Brooklyn, but a solemn high mass of requiem was celebrated at St. James Roman Catholic Church in Red Bank. Ironically, the name of the officiating priest was Rev. John B. McCloskey!

Vaudeville may have faded away, but the influence of its great stars on today's entertainment never dies.

A 1922 portrait of Maggie Cline in her quieter, later years by Otto
Sarony. The illustrious Irish vaudeville singer lived in Red Bank
and in Fair Haven where she died in 1934. *Moss Archives.*

Act IV
Highlands and
Atlantic Highlands

The picturesque towns of Highlands and Atlantic Highlands attracted theatrical people, artists, and writers who found summer retreats there, so near and yet seemingly so far from New York City. Starting in the first half of the nineteenth century, steamboats made frequent trips from the city to both towns and in the early 1890s, changes and improvements in rail service helped to make these areas even easier to reach. Gradually, like many other shore towns, the numerous hotels and summer bungalows gave way to more permanent homes.

The Twin Lights, built in 1862, and the Highlands hills with boats sailing by and a houseboat in the foreground, c. 1900. A colony of actors, artists and writers lived in homes near the lighthouses, many with water views of Sandy Hook and of New York City on a clear day.

A Female Impersonator – Neil Burgess

"...a big man without the slightest trace of good looks, [who] could, without difficulty, seem the woman he was playing, whether making a pie in the kitchen, giving a piece of her mind to an interfering interloper or starting a young couple on the way to matrimony. Nothing of the effect, somewhat unpleasing, that one associates with the young 'female impersonator' of vaudeville inhered in Burgess's wholesome, jolly characterizations." George C.D. Odell, as quoted in *The Oxford Companion to American Theater*

When America's foremost female impersonator, Neil Burgess, moved to the Highlands hills in 1883, curious locals may have been disappointed not to see him walking around in a dress and wig. Burgess was an actor who achieved great success burlesquing female roles, particularly widows and older women, but offstage he led the life of a conventional Victorian family man. Burgess was an enterprising individual who invested in theatrical endeavors as well as real estate at the New Jersey shore. He was an investor who was willing to take some chances.

Right:
A prominent resident of the Highlands hills, Neil Burgess was best known to Victorian audiences as a female impersonator. This vintage cigar box label provides a portrait of the actor in street clothes and scenes from two of his humorous roles as older "Widdy" women. Eye-catching color lithographs of famous people were prevalent on cigar boxes in the late nineteenth and early twentieth centuries and are collectible today.

His Early Career

Burgess was born in Boston in 1846 (or 1851) and was said to have given up an art business for a career on the stage. He made his debut in a variety show with Spalding's Bell Ringers in 1865, and he first performed in New York at Tony Pastor's theater in a solo act that would now be considered offensive as an "Ethiopian Comedian." alongside Edwin Booth and Lawrence Barrett.

As the story goes, Burgess had to replace the female lead at a Providence theater unexpectedly one night after the actress became ill. He began appearing as a female impersonator at New York's Theater Comique in 1877. Within a few years, he had found his niche playing elderly women.

Widdy Women

Burgess was well known as the title character of *Widow Bedott* who was a popular character for many years. The actor would play this part and other "widdy women," as they were called, throughout the rest of his career. Making its debut in New York on March 5, 1889, *The County Fair* attracted family audiences and instantly became a big

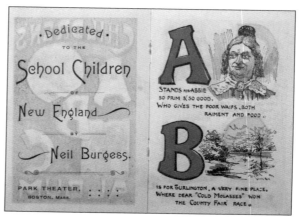

In the 1890s, little "ABC" books were given to children who went to see the play *County Fair*, set in Burlington, Massachusetts. Neil Burgess, actor and famous female impersonator who lived in Highlands, produced the show and played Abbie Prue, the prim woman shown by the letter "A."

hit for Burgess. In this down-home production "Endorsed by Press, Pulpit and Public," Burgess portrayed Aunt Abby Prue, a prissy "old maid" who aids homeless waifs. The play, written especially for Burgess by Charles Barnard, takes place at a rural fair ground in Burlington, Massachusetts. Americans loved the show but when Burgess took it to England, it was panned by British audiences.

Entrepreneur Burgess

Besides being one of America's most popular entertainers, Burgess designed mechanical devices that were used for special effects on stage. Horses often appeared in plays and ways were needed to make it look as if the equine actors were running, especially in scenes such as the horse race in *The County Fair*. Burgess patented several machines that created spectacular illusions of movement. With the advent of motion pictures, his contraptions were no longer as exciting or profitable as they were in earlier times. He also invested money to create an apparatus to simulate the sound of a crowd for which he received a patent in 1905.

Burgess also invested in real estate. He purchased land on Navesink Avenue in the Highlands hills to the west of the old hotels near the bridge, and had a house built where he and his wife Mary lived. The mansion constructed in 1883, with turrets and a tower, was designed from plans by architects Charles and George Palliser, well known for their Victorian pattern books. Burgess named the somewhat monstrous-looking house "Tempus Fugit" meaning "time flies" in Latin. The actor bought additional land in Highlands hoping to make some big profits from an unanticipated real estate boom in the area. Around 1891, he purchased more than a dozen acres for $7,500 (a huge amount in those days) that extended from Navesink Avenue (Route 36) to the Shrewsbury River, at Rogers and N. Linden Avenues.[1]

Hard Times

Burgess fell upon hard times and increasingly relied upon his mother-in-law Ann Stoddard of the famous Stoddard acting family to help him out. When his wife Mary died in 1905, Burgess was devastated. He tried to keep going with his career, taking a scaled down version of *The Country Fair* on vaudeville circuits, but the audiences had developed different tastes by then. Neil Burgess, once America's favorite "widdy woman" died at his New York City home from diabetes in 1910. He was buried at All Saints Episcopal Church in Navesink, not far from his house where a family monument with an imposing bust of the star presides over the Highlands Hills.

A formidable bust of actor Neil Burgess who lived in Highlands tops the monument of his family grave in Navesink.

The Jolly Troubadour – Nellie McHenry

"Nellie McHenry is the best eccentric soubrette on the stage. She can sing even better than she used to, she can act any thing from straight business to burlesque, she dances with a comic art that is rare. She does a great deal of work, clean, vivacious, enlivening work without a single dull or stupid movement in her whole performance." *The Trenton Times,* April 25, 1889

Nellie McHenry in costume for her role in *The Hummingbird,* a popular comedy presented by Nate Salsbury's Troubadours in the 1870s. The portrait captures the star's delightful sassiness. Nellie and her husband John Webster, also a member of the Troubadours, lived in Monmouth County's Highlands Hills on Portland Road.

Jolly Good Fun

There's no doubt from all the great reviews she received that "Jolly Nellie McHenry" could charm any audience, even the stuffiest of Victorian crowds. Born on May 29, 1853, in St. Louis, Nellie acted with the greatest stars of the classical stage. In the early days of her career, she appeared alongside Edwin Booth and Lawrence Barrett. In the early 1870s she worked with the famous Hooley Company in Chicago where she met Nate Salsbury. He started up a stock comedy company called "The Troubadours" with McHenry and actor John Webster as the leading players. Salsbury's wife was also in the company. In 1883, Salsbury went on to become partners with the legendary William F. Cody as co-owner of Buffalo Bill's Wild West show. But before that, in the 1870s, Salsbury achieved great success with his Troubadours, and Nellie became one of America's favorite comedy stars.

Perhaps the Troubadours best-known production was *The Brook*; or *A Jolly Day at the Picnic*, a play that is said to be the landmark beginning of American musical theater. Other big hits for the Troubadours included a farce called *The Hummingbird* and a backstage romp called *Green Room Fun*. Nellie married John Webster and the Troubadours toured all over America, Canada, Europe and Australia. They were innovative for their time and the public loved their witty, fast paced original work.

An delightful die cut card, c. 1870s, advertises young Nellie McHenry in *Lady Peggy* "with its realistic scene, The Old Boat House."

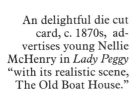

Biker Girl

The Troubadours were a hard act to follow, as the old saying goes. Nevertheless, after the troupe disbanded, Nellie had no problem finding work. She starred in the spectacular *A Night at the Circus* in 1891, playing both roles of twins who were big top performers. In 1895, Nellie McHenry produced *The Bicycle Girl*, "a musical and acrobatic farce" about the hottest craze of the 1890s. Bicycling was a growing form of exercise for women and the sport gave them new found freedom as one journal put it, "to dress and act like men." The play opened in New York, went on tour and was well-liked in San Francisco.

A Mystery at Niagara Falls

Nellie and John Webster lived well at their large house in the Highland hills on Portland Road, near the Twin Lights. The Websters entertained local theatrical friends and participated in community events. Then, a dreadful incident occurred. The details remain a mystery, but around 1900, John Webster disappeared one night while at Niagara Falls, apparently having plunged over the falls to his death, but his body was never found.[1]

The Show Must Go On

Nellie suffered from the news of her husband's unexplained (and presumed) death but continued to act. Now in her fifties, she appeared in plays, including *The Merry Wives of Windsor* that was the grand opening performance at Frick's Lyceum in Red Bank. Eventually, she retired from the theater and kept the house in the Highlands hills and also owned a residence in Brooklyn, New York. She died on May 3, 1935, at "Dr. Hazard's Sanitarium," Long Branch, shortly before her eighty-second birthday. Sadly, the once jolly Nellie was penniless, and her funeral expenses were paid by the Actors Fund of America.

Former Highlands Mayor John Bud Bahr recalled his next-door-neighbor, Nellie McHenry Webster, as "walking down the hill, in full theatrical costume, en route to the open-air theater which was located in the Waterwitch section of Highlands."[2] There's no denying that theatrical stars make memorable neighbors.

The Romantic Farmer and his Wives – Robert B. Mantell

A Shakespearian Who Grew Strawberries

"Last season was all right and if all goes well we'll see you in Frisco next season about 7th Feb. Our place is looking fine. We have the biggest strawberries that were ever grown, as big as turkey eggs. I have four horses, two cows, over 100 hens, pigeons by the dozen. What do you think of that for an actor?"

So wrote the great tragedian Robert Bruce Mantell about farming at his country estate in Atlantic Highlands, New Jersey, in a letter to Hamilton Dobbin, an Irish school chum and lifelong friend. Dobbin lived in San Francisco where he worked for the police department.

Farming was a source of pride and enjoyment but Mantell's main business was theater and his life revolved around acting. In the early twentieth century, he toured the country with his repertory company taking Shakespearean plays and other classics to audiences in every imaginable space from lavish city opera houses to small town school auditoriums.

The great Shakespearean actor Robert B. Mantell enjoyed playing the real life "role" of a gentleman farmer at his country retreat, Brucewood, on Avenue D in Atlantic Highlands. This photo taken in his cornfield appeared in *The Theatre* magazine in 1906.

Mantell's Early Life

On February 7, 1854, Robert Bruce Mantell was born at a tavern in Ayrshire, Scotland, known as The Wheatsheaf Inn and owned by his parents, James and Elizabeth Bruce Mantell. When Robert was five years old, his parents decided that The Wheatsheaf Inn was too small, and moved their growing family to Belfast. There they took over a hotel that had a bad reputation but they soon turned it into a respectable place. Robert went to several schools in Belfast and his first job was at the age of fourteen when he was apprentice to a wholesale liquor dealer, but he wanted to be an actor. He joined an amateur drama club and in 1873, he was cast in the play *Richelieu* at the Theater Royal in Belfast.

Coming to America

At first, Mantell used the stage name "Robert Hudson" so he would not disgrace his family name during an era when actors were generally not respected. In 1870, he had traveled to America for a brief stay. Mantell returned to the United States in 1878 and landed a role in *Romeo and Juliet,* playing Romeo to the Juliet of the beautiful Polish-born star, Mme. Helena Modjeska.

A Sarony cabinet card portrait of Robert B. Mantell c.1880 as Loris Ipanoff in the popular drama *Fedora* that starred Fanny Davenport. The role established the Scottish born Mantell as a leading romantic actor in America.

He began using his real name again for his stage career and never returned to using the name "Hudson." He returned briefly to Great Britain and then soon revisited the United States to play the leading role of Loris Ipanoff in *Fedora* (1883) starring the enchanting Fanny Davenport. Mantell went on to star in other popular romantic plays including *Tangled Lives, The Marble Heart, The Corsican Brothers* and the popular *Monbars,* a swashbuckling play about a pirate.

After 1900, he starred almost exclusively in Shakespearean roles playing Hamlet, Macbeth, Romeo, Brutus, Richard III, Shylock, Orlando and more. Some critics put down his "thundering" old fashioned style. Nevertheless, Mantell attracted large audiences and seemed undaunted by reviewers.

Wᴹ A. BRADY
PRESENTS:-

MR. MANTELL
AS
SHYLOCK

Robert B. Mantell of Atlantic Highlands makes an impressive Shylock on this promotional card for *The Merchant of Venice,* c.1915. Mantell's manager at that time was William D. Brady, who summered in Allenhurst where he also managed prizefighters.

The Four Wives of Robert B. Mantell

Although a professional and disciplined performer, Mantell personified the dashing and incurable romantic both onstage and off. Nevertheless, he was not known to be a philanderer. His four wives were also his leading ladies and two of them whom he loved dearly did not survive him. His initial marriage proved to be the only unhappy one.

Enter Marie Sheldon

Mantell's first marriage was to actress Marie Sheldon, in the early 1880s. Marie was born Marie Shand in Scotland. She had appeared with her husband in the American debut of the popular drama *Fedora* by Victorien Sardou.

Little is known about the troubled marriage that resulted in an unpleasant divorce in 1893 and made headlines. Marie eventually sued him for not paying alimony. She won her case and was awarded an allowance in the amount of one hundred dollars a week.

Robert Mantell protested, refused to pay, and there was a warrant out for his arrest. Somehow he managed to escape the law, but he was not allowed to perform in New York for almost ten years, a situation that was a difficult blow to his acting career. Nevertheless, his resilient nature would keep him touring. Robert B. Mantell and Marie Sheldon had two sons, Robert Shand Mantell and Jack Parcher Mantell. They tried acting but without success. Robert became a businessman in Detroit, and Jack was also in business but in New York.

Enter Charlotte Behrens

It wasn't long before Mantell fell in love and married another of his leading ladies. She was Charlotte Behrens (1866-1898), an exquisite beauty, born in Brooklyn, New York, who got her start acting in San Francisco when she was only sixteen. Interestingly, Marie Sheldon and Charlotte knew each other and had even acted together in several plays with Mantell. Charlotte and Mantell were married in just one day after her divorce from a theatrical manager who publicly threatened Mantell's life. Charlotte was pregnant with Mantell's child when they married on December 29, 1895. Sadly, at the age of thirty- two, Charlotte became ill and died at Port Huron, Michigan when little Ethel was only three years old.

Morrison HAYMARKET THEATRE BLDG.
161 WEST MADISON ST.
CHICAGO.

The lovely leading lady Charlotte Behrens toured in romantic plays during the late nineteeth century. She became Robert B. Mantell's second wife in 1896. Tragically, Charlotte died when their baby daughter Ethel was only three years old. *Courtesy of Laurie Sisson.*

Enter Marie Booth Russell

Mantell was devastated but determined to make a good life for his daughter, and he needed to marry someone who would be understanding of his theatrical lifestyle. He made a big comeback when he could finally act in New York again. In 1900, Mantell married yet another of his leading ladies, a tall and somewhat hefty actress from Brooklyn with a compassionate nature. Her name was Marie Booth Russell. Marie had a child by a short-lived previous marriage, a daughter named Louise, who was about the same age as Mantell's daughter Ethel. The children got along fabulously together.

Mantell and his bride began house hunting for a summer place in Monmouth County as it was convenient to New York and the theater district. They discovered the beauty of Atlantic Highlands during the summer of 1901.

Right:
Marie Booth Russell, Robert B. Mantell's third wife and a leading lady, is the subject of this Rotograph real photo card, c.1905. Mantell and Marie purchased a farmhouse, first known as Cherrywood and renamed Brucewood, on Avenue D in Atlantic Highlands in 1906. Marie died at Brucewood on Halloween 1911.

MARIE BOOTH RUSSELL

Brucewood

Around 1908, Mantell and Marie purchased the rustic home called "Cherrywood" at West Highland Avenue and Avenue D. The house was originally built about 1863 by James H. Leonard, who had purchased the Debow farm. Within a few years, Mantell would rename the property "Brucewood" (for the Scottish hero Robert Bruce, and his own middle name) and he acquired an adjacent parcel of open land that he called "Maywood" (Marie was sometimes called "May.")

Mantell made renovations to the house, adding porches and other structural changes. On the lush grounds, he planted many varieties of shrubs and added touches such as a grape arbor and a hand hewn rustic fence. It is said that Mantell, who enjoyed woodworking, constructed the fence himself.

The house has a center hall, two fireplaces one of which is made of rustic stone, and several bathrooms. The bedrooms were small but charming with lots of windows and closets. A door led from the master bedroom to a balcony that overlooked the garden of roses, lilacs, lilies, hydrangeas, irises, rhododendrons, and mountain laurel.

A small building near the main house served as a space where the Mantells could rehearse plays with their repertory company. The building was known simply as "The Studio." There was also a stone well at Brucewood that was said to be copied after one at Shakespeare's birthplace, Stratford on Avon. A large barn housed elaborate scenery and backdrops. The splendid holly on the north side of the house, said to be planted by Mantell himself, remains to date and has been designated as a historic tree.

The Mantell home in Atlantic Highlands c. 1907. The photo for this postcard was taken before the actor remodeled the house, although it appears that an addition to the east side (right) was already added. He made major changes to the simple colonial home that was built in the early 1860s by James H. Leonard.

Enjoying a summer afternoon at Brucewood in 1910 are Robert B. Mantell, his wife Marie Booth Russell, their daughters Ethel and Louise (in hammock on right), and the family dog, "Rubber." *The Ladies World,* September 1910.

A Dormitory for Actors

The Mantell repertory actors would arrive in May at the end of the theatrical season and visit throughout the summer, rehearsing plays until the theaters opened in September. The atmosphere was one of great camaraderie for players enjoyed getting away from the heat of the City in summer. Mantell had the top floor of the house converted from an attic into a finished space with dormer windows, bedrooms and bathrooms.

The neighbors seemed to accept the theatrical family and their guests as neighbors, perhaps because the Mantells contributed much to the community. During the summer months, besides rehearsing with their company, Mr. and Mrs. Mantell conducted summer acting classes for local girls that their own daughters participated in.

A c. 1912 postcard of Brucewood, the Atlantic Highlands home of actor Robert B. Mantell, on Avenue D, shows the addition of a top floor "dormitory" for the actors of his company including a Dutch colonial roof with dormers. The wrap-around verandah was added to the main floor. Striped awnings and a lawn tennis net complete the picture. The house, now The St. Agnes Thrift Shop, is still intact.

Benefit Performances

In the summer of 1910, William Brady, a manager of theatrical and boxing stars who had a home in Allenhurst, produced a performance of *As You Like It* for the benefit of St. Mary's Roman Catholic

Church in Deal. An elaborate production presented outdoors, the play featured Marie Booth Russell as Rosalind, Mantell as Orlando, Fritz Leiber as Jacques and Virginia Bronson as Phoebe. Bronson was Leiber's wife and the couple bought a house in Atlantic Highlands, close to Mantell.

The Mantell Company was involved with the community and did their best to be good neighbors. At the request of Atlantic Highlands pharmacist Ira Antonides, the Mantell troupe gave a benefit performance to raise money for a new fire truck for the town. On a warm night in August 1911, the show took place at the old open air Lyric Theater on First Avenue.[1] The performance raised enough money for the town to purchase its first motorized fire truck. On October 16, 1911, the Grand View Hose Co., No. 2, incorporated in 1893, officially changed its name to The Robert B. Mantell Hose Company.

Photographed with their troupe at Denver, Colorado, Fritz Leiber (center) and his wife Virginia Bronson were prominent Shakespearean actors in The Mantell Company. They lived in Atlantic Highlands across from Brucewood, but had a falling out with Mantell and started their own repertory company in 1920. The new troupe was based at first in Atlantic Highlands and then in Leiber's hometown, Chicago. Fritz Leiber became a successful film actor, starring as Caesar in *Cleopatra* (1917) with Theda Bara, and played in movies until his death in 1949. Leiber's son, Fritz Leiber Jr., (probably the boy wearing knickers in photo) became a world famous science fiction and fantasy writer. Atlantic Highlands Historical Society.

Halloween of 1911

Except for the summer months, The Mantells toured making stops all over the country and often performing a different play each night. It was a grueling schedule and after Marie became ill in the spring of 1911, she could not continue the tour with her husband that Fall. She stayed at the quiet country retreat in Altantic Highlands to rest and recuperate.

While Mantell was continuing with the tour, he received a telegram that Marie was weakening and he rushed back to Atlantic Highlands to see his beloved wife, reaching home on that eerie night of Halloween, October 31, 1911. There were some conflicting stories about his time of arrival but the *New York Times* reported that she died soon after her husband arrived. Marie Booth Russell succumbed to Bright's disease complicated by pneumonia. She was laid to rest at Bay View Cemetery just a few miles from Brucewood.

Mantell was crushed at the loss of Marie. His loneliness did not last long, for he continued with his company of actors and very soon yet another beautiful leading lady, who had already graced his company on stage, would become the leading woman in his life.

Enter Genevieve Hamper

The pretty dark-haired ingénue who stepped in to console Robert Mantell was Genevieve Hamper, an upstart and protégé of Marie Booth Russell. Genevieve, a farm girl from the Greenville, Michigan, area, got her theatrical start in 1910 by waiting in line for a job as an extra for a musical in Detroit. Her classic beauty and sensational singing voice soon were noticed and she was asked to tryout for the Mantell Company. She was cast in a minor role by Robert Mantell and Marie Booth Russell.

Right:
The Forest of Arden? Under a canopy of trees at Brucewood, her Atlantic Highlands home, Genevieve Hamper Mantell posed as Rosalind from Shakespeare's As You Like It. This photo that appeared on a vintage postcard was also reproduced as a stunning cover for *The Theatre* magazine's June 1921 issue.

"As You Like It"
Miss Genevieve Hamper as "Rosalind"

Less than three months after Marie Booth Russell's death, Robert B. Mantell and Genevieve Hamper were married in a hushed ceremony by a Justice of the Peace, in Pueblo, Colorado, on January 16, 1912. Twenty-three-year-old Genevieve, who looked even younger,

Robert B. Mantell as "Romeo"
Miss Genevieve Hamper as "Juliet"

became the fourth wife of fifty-four-year-old star Robert. Within a few years, she was playing leading roles, including Juliet, Desdemona, Ophelia, Portia, Rosalind, and Lady Macbeth in the Mantell Hamper repertory company.

The Next Great Tragedian Is Born

Eight months after their marriage, a son was born to Genevieve and Robert Mantell. They named the healthy boy Robert Bruce, Jr. His father, who was often mistaken for the child's grandfather, doted on his son. Genevieve's mother raised the baby, as it was too difficult to take him on the grueling tours. Genevieve and Robert appeared at theaters in Boston, New York, Atlanta, St. Louis, New Orleans, Denver, San Francisco, San Diego, Portland, and many other cities, do-

ing one or two shows almost every day. Whenever they had time off and during the summer season, they always returned to their only permanent home, Brucewood, where they would spend time with their son. Genevieve missed him terribly while they were traveling, but she had to work; a repertory star had to be on the road.

A tender 1913 photo of Robert B. Mantell and his son "Baby Bruce," whose mother was Genevieve Hamper. *Robert Mantell's Romance*, 1918.

Left:
The tragedian Robert B. Mantell and his fourth wife Genevieve Hamper, residents of Atlantic Highlands, make an appealing *Romeo and Juliet* as captured in the photo on this c.1917 promotional postcard. Mantell was still playing the youthful role of Romeo to his much younger wife/leading lady when he was in his early sixties.

The Silent Screen

In 1915-1916, Robert and Genevieve took time off from their hectic touring schedule to make silent movies. They signed on with William Fox, who had a studio at Fort Lee, New Jersey, the center of filmmaking in its early days. The six silent films they made for Fox were contemporary society dramas, not Shakespearean plays. Mantell, who depended upon his booming voice, didn't do well with films, but Genevieve was offered starring roles in the movies. Although told she could be the next Theda Bara, she declined and continued to tour the country with her husband and their highly regarded Shakespearean and classical repertory. In 1923, they made one more film, *Under the Red Robe*, for Hearst's Cosmopolitan pictures. It was based on the story of Cardinal Richelieu, one of Mantell's favorite stage roles.

Appearances in Monmouth County

During World War I, Robert and Genevieve continued to appear throughout the United States and Canada, adding Shakespeare's *King John* to their repertory. They did not travel overseas, but entertained American troops at home. In Camp Vail's (later Fort Monmouth) newspaper, *Dots & Dashes*, the Mantells are mentioned as entertaining troops there on in the summer of 1918. In the late 1920s, they appeared at local Monmouth County theaters more frequently, as Robert's health began to decline.

The Final Scene

Robert B. Mantell performed until just a few months before his death. The great tragedian's last performance in Monmouth County was on September, 1927, at the Savoy in Asbury Park. Mantell died at Brucewood on June 27, 1928, at the age of 74. He had suffered a "breakdown" while on a tour, and returned home to be with his family. Private funeral services were held at Brucewood. The Robert B. Mantell Hose Company's truck, acquired thanks to the great actor, accompanied his body to his burial site nearby at Bay View Cemetery.

Moving On

Genevieve Hamper mourned for Mantell, but at age thirty-nine she needed to move on with her life and career. A few months after Mantell's death, she secretly married actor John Alexander, who was considerably younger than she and had been a leading member of the Mantell troupe. Genevieve started her own Shakespearean touring company with John at her side. They appeared on the Chautauqua circuits, but the hard economic times of the Great Depression relegated her troupe to performances at school auditoriums and second-rate theaters.

In his final years, Robert B. Mantell and Genevieve Hamper performed their Shakespearean repertory in Monmouth County more often. The aging Mantell who had toured all over the United States and Canada for so many years probably needed to stay closer to his Atlantic Highlands home at the time of this 1927 performance at Reade's Broadway Theatre (later to become The Paramount) at Long Branch.

READE'S

Broadway Theatre

Long Branch, N. J.

Saturday Matinee, Sept. 17, 1927.

"As You Like It"

By William Shakespeare

CAST

JAQUES	MR. MANTELL
Banished Duke	Mr. Bruce Adams
Oliver	Mr. John Forrest
Orlando	Mr. John Alexander
Adam	Mr. John C. Hickey
Duke Frederick	Mr. Frederic W. Hile
Jaques DeBois	Mr. Deaver Storer
Sylvius	Mr. Frederic W. Hile
Corin	Mr. James Hendrickson
LeBeau	Mr. John Schellhaas
Second Lord	Mr. Charles Keane
Celia	Miss Mary Glover
Phoebe	Miss Claire Bruce
Touchstone	Mr. Edward LeDuc
William	Mr. John Schellhaas
Charles	Mr. James Alexander
First Lord	Mr. Edwin Foss
Amiens	Mr. Rex Keith
Audrey	Miss Sarah Alexander
ROSALIND	MISS GENEVIEVE HAMPER

PLACE OF ACTION—Scene, France

Act 1.—Scene 1— Oliver's Orchard. Scene 2— A Lawn Before the Duke's Palace.

Act 2.—Scene 1—Oliver's Garden. Scene 2—The Forest of Arden. Scene 3—Another Part of the Forest. Scene 4—The Forest of Arden.

Act 3.—Scene—The Forest of Arden.

Act 4.—The Same.

Act 5.—Scene 1—The Forest. Scene 2 Another Part of the Forest.

Real Life Tragedy

To make ends meet, in 1931, Genevieve was forced to sell Brucewood and auction off the furnishings, as well as costumes and sets. A fire occurred shortly before the scheduled auction, destroying the barn and theatrical items that were stored there. After Genevieve sold Brucewood, she moved to Hollywood, where John was becoming popular in films as a character actor. Now, Genevieve was unable to secure work in the movies. In 1933, her only child, Robert Bruce Mantell, Jr., committed suicide at the age of twenty-one. Devastated by his death, Genevieve left the stage. She lived a secretive life in New York and died in 1971 at the age of eighty-two.[2]

The Mantell Legacy

Although Robert B. Mantell's name is no longer familiar to most people, he deserves recognition for his outstanding contributions to American theater for over fifty years. He kept Shakespearean and classical drama alive, bringing it to many people throughout the country.

Mantell's descendants have followed the family tradition of working in creative fields. Robert B. Mantell was a great uncle to Angela Lansbury, the now-famous film and television star. His daughter, Ethel Mantell Platky, did some acting in early films and was a talented painter and lived in Atlantic Highlands. She died in 1942.

The main house at Brucewood is still standing. It was a family home for many years, then was acquired by The St. Agnes Parish in the 1960s. The St. Agnes School occupies much of the property now and the house has been their thrift shop since 1968.

Act V - Around Asbury Park

Piety and Performance

"On cloudy nights there is always one star in the sky over Asbury Park. This star is James A. Bradley." Stephen Crane, 1896

The "star" that young Crane referred to mockingly was not an actor or a musician, he was the moralizing and eccentric man who founded Asbury Park, which he also ran for over thirty years. In the late nineteenth century, Stephen Crane (1871-1900) was living in Asbury Park and working as a cub reporter for The New York Tribune's local agency, which was managed by his brother, Townley. Crane, author of *The Red Badge of Courage*, was born in Newark, New Jersey.

Bradley's Vision

This story has been told many times. In 1871, a prosperous brush manufacturer from New York City, James A. Bradley, founded Asbury Park, a city of his own design. The previous year, Bradley, a convert to Methodism, had visited the Methodist camp meeting community of Ocean Grove and was impressed by its healthy qualities with invigorating air and salt water. He purchased 500 acres directly north of Ocean Grove and named the area after the founder of Methodism in America, Bishop Francis Asbury. Bradley's vision was to create an ideal, morally sound, Christian, white, middle-class resort. Its beachfront and amusements would be controlled by the city government, which was Bradley himself.

A wonderful view of Asbury Park from an 1897 souvenir booklet published by J. Murray Jordan of Philadelphia. The scene features the area on Wesley Lake across from Ocean Grove with the old Palace Merry Go Round building, crystal maze, Ferris wheel, and canopied tourist boats.

The City Beautiful

Bradley's Asbury Park featured grids of east-west avenues, parks, and fine public buildings, as well as incredibly good sanitation and electrical systems. Although James Bradley was responsible for many positive improvements, he ran the place like a puppet master. Although he showed concern for the health and welfare of the people, the concepts of religious tolerance and racial equality unfortunately were not part of his agenda.

By 1875, the extended railroad brought more day trippers to the New Jersey coast and to Asbury Park. Besides the thousands of daily visitors, Asbury Park became a vacation destination. Despite strict bans on alcohol and gambling, boarding houses and hotels popped up all over the city. Band concerts, the annual baby parade and carnival (started in 1890), a merry-go-round, an observation wheel, shops, and eventually theaters attracted the public to the growing resort.

Acceptable Entertainment

Methodists in the 19th century frowned upon the popular theater and its allegedly irreverent actors. Nevertheless, there were theatrical

performers who visited Asbury Park for rest and relaxation, probably not announcing their occupations too loudly. Though itinerant
acts and musicians could be seen on the boardwalk, theaters were
not allowed in the town originally. In Asbury Park's early days,
vacationers attended programs at Educational Hall, a building that
Bradley moved from the 1876 Centennial Exposition in Philadelphia
to Grand Avenue between First and Second Avenues. There was also
the 2,500-seat Asbury Park Auditorium that Bradley owned at Sunset
and Ocean Avenues, and another privately owned 1,500-seat Opera
House was at Bangs Avenue and Emory Street. Although bookings
at these venues in the late 1800s included light opera companies,
variety acts, and cakewalkers, the "entertainment" was often in the
form of moral and self-improvement lectures.

INTERIOR OF AUDITORIUM, SHOWING THE LARGEST ORGAN IN THE WORLD. OCEAN GROVE, N. J.

A 1920s postcard of the interior of the Ocean Grove auditorium and "the largest organ
in the world." The gargantuan hall, used for religious services and concerts is still in use
today. Asbury Park's neighbor to the south, Ocean Grove (Township of Neptune), was
founded in the 1860s as a Methodist camp meeting and tent community. Built in 1894
and replacing its rustic open-air predecessors, the new hall could seat 10,000 people and
hosted sermons, lectures, and concerts. Great opera stars, renowned orchestras, choirs,
John Philip Sousa's band, speakers such as black leader and educator Booker T. Washington, and several U.S. Presidents have appeared at the Ocean Grove auditorium. Over
the years, a variety of stars have performed there including Bob Hope, Tony Bennett, The
Preservation Hall Jazz Band, and Peter, Paul and Mary.

The Sporting Life

Sporting events were considered more acceptable than theatrical amusements. Bradley's Asbury Park was meant to be a place for healthy rejuvenation, so athletic activities go as far back as the 1880s, including roller skating, swimming, tennis, amateur baseball, and football were promoted. Bicycling was all the rage in the late 19th century and vacationers enjoyed riding on the bike path along the oceanfront at Asbury Park. Bicycling also became a competitive sport and in 1895, the city hosted the national meet of the League of American Wheelman. Of course, gambling was taboo, but many spectator sports got the seal of approval from founder Bradley.

Gentleman Jim

Boxing was popular in late 19th century America and one of its great stars, James J. Corbett, trained around Asbury Park. Known as "Gentlemen Jim," he won the heavy weight title from John L. Sullivan in 1892. According to Stephen Crane, Corbett's "gentlemanly behavior and quiet manners" charmed the locals. The versatile Corbett even appeared in vaudeville, early movies including a landmark 1894 Edison film, and later was heard on radio. The pugilist's manager, William A. Brady, a shrewd entrepreneur, also managed actors including Robert B. Mantell, who was an excellent amateur boxer and knew the importance of creating a good image for boxing. Brady, who had a home in Allenhurst, opened a film production company, and was the father of Alice Brady who became a well known movie star.

End of a Regime

Although Bradley lived until 1921, his control ended when he relinquished ownership of the oceanfront to the city of Asbury Park in 1903. The field was open for more theaters. In 1903, a necktie salesman from Alabama, Walter Rosenberg, a nephew of Oscar Hammerstein I, acquired the Rialto, a small vaudeville house on Main Street. The storefront theater's patrons were mostly from the immigrant population of the West Side. As the first decade of the 20th century came to a close, construction began on new theaters. They would become lucrative attractions for the resort that now wanted to cater to modern tastes. The theater had evolved as an acceptable pastime and the entertainment business was going through amazing changes with exciting new inventions.

When the "talkies" began in the late 1920s, movie "palaces" were constructed and theaters designed for live shows became less important. By the 1930s, "going to the theater" usually meant a movie for most suburbanites.

A couple of guys from Jersey, better known as Abbott and Costello. William Alexander Abbott, was born in Asbury Park in 1895. He is better known as Bud Abbott, "straight man" of the Abbott and Costello comedy team. One of their best-known routines was the hilarious "Who's on first?" Lou Costello was born in Paterson in 1906. The Abbott family left Asbury Park to join a circus not long after Bud was born. His father was as an advance man and his mother performed as a bareback rider. Bud Abbott dropped out of school and worked in carnivals until, by luck, he met Lou Costello in 1931. The Jersey-born duo teamed up, and starred in vaudeville, films, radio and television for almost thirty years. They often made appearances in their home state. Costello died in 1959 and Abbott in 1974.

Theater Tales

The saga of the Savoy Theater, that opened in 1912 on Mattison Avenue, reflects what happened to many legitimate theaters during the 20th century. The Savoy was a theater set within the Kinmonth office building and it was first leased by Walter Rosenberg. It proved to be at a prime location for live plays and musicals. Performances ranged from *The Secret Service*, a drama with Sydney Greenstreet, to *The Darktown Follies of 1914*, a Shubert musical revue, to *The Spring Maid*, a popular operetta. In 1915, the Savoy began to offer silent movies as well as live performances. The feature film for the week of July 20, 1919, was *Broken Blossoms* with Lillian Gish. There was a Savoy Stock Company in the 1920s that put on live shows soon after they completed their New York runs.

From 1931 to 1950, the Savoy was used as a movie theater and was well attended. In the 1950s, it offered burlesque shows and some summer theater productions. Then, its sad decline intensified. When the Savoy shut down in 1976, it was operating as a pornographic movie house. On the bright side, the historic Savoy remains intact today and may be restored as a center for the arts, but its fate is undecided at the time of this writing.

The Ocean Theater on Fourth Avenue dates back to 1913. It was taken over by the Sunset Hall Hotel next door as an auxiliary building, but when the huge Asbury Park fire of 1917 destroyed the hotel, the theater, with its state of the art fireproofing for its day, survived. It even helped to stop the blaze from spreading to the rest of the block. The Ocean Theater was purchased by Walter Reade in 1949 as a movie house and renamed the Baronet. In the mid 1980s, new owners restored it to its 1950s-60s appearance. Threatened with extinction, the Baronet under new management successfully reopened in 2006.

The Lyric, first opened in 1912 as a vaudeville house, was on Cookman Avenue adjacent to the celebrated Palace Amusements and the ever-smiling, painted face of "Tillie." A wrecking ball knocked down the Palace Amusements in 2004, and the Lyric was toppled in 2005. In its final years, the Lyric, renamed The Park, had a triple "x" displayed prominently with clear meaning of the films being shown. The moral Mr. Bradley would have been shocked by this type of entertainment in his ideal city.

A program for the professional Savoy Stock Company that put on plays during the 1920s at the Mattison Ave. theater located within the Kinmonth building. *In the Wrong Bed*, a popular comedy of the day set in Pine Beach, New Jersey, was first seen in New York. *Moss Archives.*

READE'S

Savoy Theatre

ASBURY PARK, N. J.

Under the personal direction of Charles J. Bryan
Walter Gutteridge, Manager

WEEK OF JANUARY 31, 1927

CHARLES J. BRYAN

presents

THE SAVOY STOCK COMPANY

in

"IN THE WRONG BED"

A Comedy in Three Acts by Bide Dudley.
As produced at the
FULTON THEATRE, NEW YORK CITY

Staged by William Webb

THE CAST

Henry Boswell	William Webb
Lizzie	Isabel Carson
John Carson	James M. Hugh
Mrs. John Carson	Anne Davis
Jennie Carson	Edna Preston
Harley West	Robert Leslie
Dave Williams	William E. Blake
Annabelle Wyngate	Dollie Davis Webb
Chauffeur	Jack Byrne
Guard	Jack Byrne

PLACE OF ACTION

Act I.　The Living room of John Carson's Bungalow, Pine Beach, N. J.
Act II.　The Same.　Thirty Minutes Later.
Act III.　The Same.　One Minute Later.

Time — Present

SUMMER

Scenic Artist	Dallas Packard
Stage Manager	Jack Byrne

— : —

Furniture by Capitol Furniture Co. and Rogers.
Electrical effects by Crowell Electric Co. and Adelman.
Novelties by Reines.
Crockery by Crockery Shop.
All Jewelry by Vogue Jewelry Shop.
Shoes by I. Miller.
Hats furnished by Juliette Marjorie Shop.

Once Upon a Time...

Two "palaces," the St. James and the Mayfair, both designed by noted theatre architect Thomas W. Lamb, who planned Madison Square Garden, occupied sites next to one another. Built in 1917 by Walter Rosenberg for $200,000, The St. James was located on the southwest corner of Cookman Avenue and St. James Place. When it opened, the theater displayed the name of "Reade."[2]

The most picturesque of the Asbury Park theaters, the Mayfair, touted as "The Palace of Spanish Art," opened in 1927. Situated alongside Wesley Lake, the off-white stucco Moorish theater occupied the corner of Lake Avenue and St. James Place.

Despite the efforts of historians and theater buffs to save them, the sister theaters did not live happily ever after. In December of 1974, the St. James and the Mayfair theaters were both demolished and the site was transformed into a parking lot.

A Landmark Today

Still standing and in use, the landmark Paramount Theater and Convention Hall is located on the northern part of the boardwalk across from Atlantic Square, where the statue of founder James Bradley faces the theater. The entertainment complex opened to the public in 1930. Designed by Beaux-Arts-trained architect Whitney Warren, of Warren and Wetmore, known for New York's Grand Central Station, this theater and hall are connected by a grand arcade. The brick façade features decorative tiles with fantasy underwater motifs, fish, shells, and garlands, and the Paramount's classic Art Deco interior has artistic details that are reminders of a bygone era in show business.

Photographs and Memories

If their walls could talk, each of the Asbury Park theaters would surely have absorbing stories to tell. Some have been razed, but memories have been kept alive by those who spent happy hours smitten by them. Hundreds of great stars appeared or were seen in movies that played at the Asbury Park theaters, and the fate of many Broadway shows was determined at tryouts here from 1920s through the 1940s.

A c. 1930 postcard view of The Mayfair at night, illustrates the magical beauty of the movie palace by Wesley Lake, a landmark from 1927 until it was demolished in 1974. Its high campanile tower had bell chimes that were controlled by the theater's giant organ. The Mayfair's interior was stunning with Spanish-inspired fixtures and decorations. The proscenium looked like a radiant sunset and the sloping ceiling resembled the sky with an illusion of clouds drifting by.

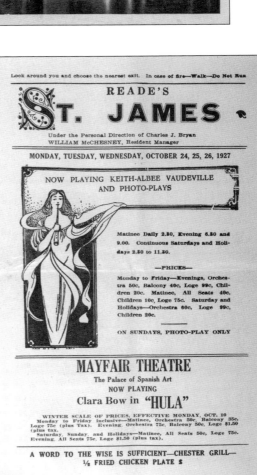

A typical 1920s program for the St. James features "vaudeville and photo plays." The theater was adjacent to the Mayfair with its entrance on Cookman Ave. Both theaters were managed by the Walter Reade organization.

The Famous Music Maker – Arthur Pryor

"I want to say for Asbury Park that while its summer population is amply supplied with every variety of alluring entertainment, its devotion to the summer concerts by Pryor's Band is inspiring." From The Musical Mecca by Arthur Pryor, published in a booklet issued by The Asbury Park Board of Trade, Asbury Park, New Jersey, 1910.

On the Boardwalk

A century ago, prim ladies wearing white lawn dresses and picture hats accompanied by dapper gents in three-piece suits and straw boaters enjoyed daily band concerts at Asbury Park's boardwalk. Underneath their tidy facades, these vacationers may have longed to let loose. Their venerated superstar was Arthur Pryor. He conducted and played traditional musical favorites and introduced them to Ragtime. When the new syncopated rhythm of Ragtime was considered off-limits for strait-laced, white, middle-class folk, Pryor gave it respectability.

Across the Tracks

Meanwhile, on Asbury Park's west side, in the segregated neighborhoods where blacks and immigrants lived, Ragtime was being played by musicians who were not accepted at the boardwalk pavilions. Many of them worked as laborers and at hotels as cooks and waiters and in other low-paid jobs. Some of them did occasionally perform where they were employed, but usually between their other duties. Their talent was admired, but they were treated as second-class citizens.

At west side clubs across the tracks, in what has been coined the "shadow city," ragtime and then blues, jazz, and swing music enthralled audiences for years. Pryor's and other white orchestra's concerts at the boardwalk remained popular from the beginning of the 20th century until around the 1930s. The jazz clubs on Springwood Avenue persevered, attracting an increasingly diverse clientele, until their decline after the Asbury Park race riots of 1970.

This boardwalk bandstand was a popular spot for Arthur Pryor's concerts at Asbury Park as seen in this detail from a 1906 Pach Brothers photograph. *Moss Archives.*

The Boy Wonder

Arthur Pryor was one of the greatest trombonists of all time, and he also achieved fame as a bandleader, composer, recording artist, and educator. Born in 1870 in St. Joseph, Missouri, his father was a bandmaster and his mother played the piano. Arthur displayed inherent musical ability as a child, developed an innovative way of playing the slide trombone, and became known as "The Boy Wonder of Missouri." After making a hit playing at local fairs, eighteen-year-old Arthur Pryor embarked on a Mid-western tour with bandleader

Allessandro Liberati, and then turned down an offer to tour with the famed Patrick S. Gilmore band. Instead, Pryor took a steady position as musical director at a vaudeville theater in Denver, Colorado, a job that gave him a diverse experience. In 1892, the celebrated "March King," John Philip Sousa, contacted Pryor and asked him to be in his new concert band. Pryor accepted the offer and, as the story goes, arrived in New York City with only thirty-five cents. But it didn't take long for Pryor to become a featured soloist in Sousa's company, and in 1895 he was promoted to Assistant Conductor. With Sousa, Pryor toured all over the United States and Europe, even performing for crowned heads of state.

Right:
Arthur Pryor, extraordinary trombonist, conductor, and composer looks smart wearing his bandleader's uniform c.1908. Pryor, who had previously played in "March King" John Philip Sousa's band, conducted boardwalk concerts with his own band at Asbury Park and was a resident of West Long Branch.

The Rise of Recordings

At the close of the nineteenth century, America was experiencing advances in industry and technology that would influence entertainment. Sousa balked at recorded music, thinking it was just a fad, and put Pryor in charge of directing the band for phonograph recording sessions. With foresight, Pryor believed that records could be profitable and would gain in popularity.

In 1903, Pryor quit Sousa's organization and decided to make it on his own as a bandleader and composer, and as musical director for the Victor Talking Machine Company, that had studios in Camden, New Jersey. He and his newly formed band went on national and international tours and played at the Saint Louis World's Fair in 1904. Though the tours were highly successful, Pryor wanted to book longer engagements at resorts, to work on theatrical productions in New York City, and to continue recording with Victor.

Arthur Pryor, Bandmaster.

Pryor's band became the resident company at Asbury Park, where they played for many seasons. They also appeared at Willow Grove Park near Philadelphia, in Florida, New York's Coney Island, and Atlantic City. Pryor's popular compositions included "On Jersey Shore" (1904) and "The Whistler and His Dog" (1905), that was used in the 1950s as the theme song for the television sitcom, "Leave It to Beaver."

The Real Rex

At Asbury Park, Pryor quickly became a superstar. His band played regular boardwalk concerts and for special events, the annual "Carnival and Baby Parade" being the most spectacular. The August festival drew huge crowds and was even compared to the New Orleans Mardi Gras. A competition was held to choose "Queen Titania" to preside over the event. In the September 1906 issue of *The Outing Magazine*, writer Charles Belmont Davis provided a lively first-hand description of "Queen Titania," as the beautiful young woman and her royal court took their places on the reviewing stand to survey the boardwalk parade:

"It took the royal party some time to get satisfactorily settled. Indeed, the merry crowd of maskers, preceded by a stirring brass band, was almost upon them before they had properly greeted their subjects.

It was just about this time that we at the Court of Honor discovered who the real hero of the fete was. Queen Titania and Prince Charming were lost in the wave of applause that greeted the real Rex of the Carnival. He was a young man with light hair and he was dressed in a dark blue suit with black braid and he wore very white kid gloves and his name, which was "Arthur," was shouted aloud by many thousands of throats until the word echoed back and forth between the sand dunes and went booming over the roughened waters of the Atlantic. And this was just as it should have been, for 'Arthur' was the leader of the band."

A photograph of the annual Baby Parade and Carnival, c. 1906. Crowds cheered for Arthur Pryor as he conducted his band at the reviewing stand for many seasons.

Arthur Pryor, the man the crowds clamored for, composed a musical piece called *Queen Titania*.

Simple Pleasures

While continuing to play at Asbury Park, Pryor spent much of his time making recordings at the Victor studios, as phonographs gained popularity and become commonplace in living-rooms across America. Pryor composed 300 original songs for recordings and became so successful and financially stable that he didn't need to perform at live concerts anymore. Simone Mantia, who had worked for Sousa and Pryor, conducted classical concerts at Asbury Park in the 1920s.

A banner for "The Pryor Band" stretched across the boardwalk passage of the Asbury Park Casino is visible in this c.1910 postcard published by Valentine & Sons. Wicker rolling chairs were not only at Atlantic City; Asbury Park had them too!

Pryor kept up a busy schedule until he retired in 1933. By that time, music had changed with new styles of dance bands and jazz combos becoming more prevalent. Although he pioneered ragtime, he did not like the growing trend for improvised jazz that had emerged from it. He referred to jazz as "the parasite of music."

After Pryor withdrew from public appearances, he and his wife, Maude (whom he married in 1895), enjoyed the simple pleasures of life on their twenty-seven acre farm, "Driftwood," the former Eaton homestead in West Long Branch. Maude liked gardening and Arthur went fishing, played billiards, and relaxed. But he also decided to fulfill a desire to do something for the community. With a platform to lower taxes, he won a seat on the Monmouth County Board of Freeholders in the 1930s and served for one term.

A 1925 program for Simone Mantia's Arcade Symphony Orchestra at the Asbury Park's Arcade Pier features a cover photo of Mantia, an Italian immigrant from Palermo who worked his way up to become regarded as one of the world's greatest euphonium players. Mantia, like Pryor, was with Sousa's band at first, then with Pryor when Pryor formed his own band. Mantia was with the Metropolitan Opera Orchestra for over thirty-five years, serving as their orchestra manager for twelve of those years.

He performed, taught music, and lived in Asbury Park and Wanamassa for most of his life. He died in 1951 at the age of 78.

ARCADE PIER

FIFTH AVE. AND BOARDWALK

ASBURY PARK, NEW JERSEY

SIMONE MANTIA, Conductor

ARCADE SYMPHONY ORCHESTRA
CONCERT EVERY AFTERNOON AND EVENING
SIMONE MANTIA, Conductor
FRIDAY EVENINGS, CHILDRENS' BALLET
DOROTHY PALMER, Director
SPECIAL ORGAN RECITALS EVERY DAY
John F. Nugent, Organist
City Management   Frederick W. Vanderpool, Mgr.

Pryor's Sons

Pryor's two sons followed in the family tradition of show business. Arthur Jr., also an accomplished musician, served as assistant conductor for the Pryor Band. He also worked as a New York advertising executive, arranging for well-known personalities to be guests on radio programs. He produced an innovative and controversial radio program called *The March of Time*, in which actors portrayed real personalities in the current news.

Pryor's younger son, Roger, was a musician and a movie actor. Roger's films were mostly Grade B productions, but he was a local hero at the New Jersey shore, as newspapers ran his photo and young women swooned over him. At one time, Roger was married to Priscilla Mitchell, the daughter of Julian Mitchell and Bessie Clayton Mitchell, but in 1936 Roger married the alluring film star Ann Sothern, and the fact that she was Arthur Pryor's daughter-in-law was often publicized. That union did not last long, and Sothern divorced Roger Pryor in 1942, saying that his love of flying constituted cruelty because she had a fear of air travel.[1]

During World War II, while German submarines prowled the New Jersey coast and blackouts were common, Arthur Pryor, then in his seventies, came out of retirement to put on patriotic concerts at Asbury Park. On Memorial Day, 1942, Pryor conducted a well attended concert. On June 17 he suffered a stroke and died at home the following day. Following the old theatrical tradition of "the show must go on," Arthur Jr. conducted the Pryor Band on the night of his father's death and concluded the program with "We'll Keep Old Glory Flying."

Arthur Pryor is buried in Glenwood Cemetery in West Long Branch, near his home. In 1962, the bandshell at Asbury Park's Fifth Avenue pavilion was named in his memory, and efforts are being made to save this structure from demolition today.

Just North of "The Park"

Several small communities immediately north of Asbury Park, including Wanamassa, Loch Arbour, Allenhurst, Interlaken, and Deal, became havens for performers, artists, and writers in the late nineteenth and early twentieth centuries. Stories of Wanamassa's famous vaudeville couple, Charlie and Mabel Ross, and Deal's once-resident opera star, Lillian Nordica, are presented next.

The Simple Life - Ross & Fenton

In the summer of 1896, a comedy actor and his wife were vacationing at Asbury Park when they took a leisurely hike and came across the area by Deal Lake called Wanamassa (Ocean Township). They immediately fell in love with the natural beauty of the countryside. Weary from years of hectic touring schedules, Charles J. (Charlie) Ross and Mabel Fenton Ross had been looking for a place to settle down. The couple was so impressed by the fragrant pine woods and serenity of Deal Lake that they were game to try the simple life.[1]

Seclusion with Accessibility

The comedy team of Ross and Fenton visited the Jersey shore several more times before deciding to invest in lakeside property in the Wanamassa woods. In 1899, they purchased their dream site but the seasoned performers were not yet ready to give up their theatrical careers. At the site of an old farm, they would not harvest vegetables, milk cows, or gather eggs, but they built an innovative bungalow resort with a classy restaurant that featured entertainment and called it "The Ross-Fenton Farm." The first bungalow erected was made of logs from trees felled on the site. Their neighbors helped to built the house at a "log cabin raising bee," just like in the Old West, as Charlie described it. The Ross-Fentons were glad to be so close to the civilized hub of Asbury Park. Ross said, "Seclusion with accessibility are two chief qualifications and in these respects Deal Lake offers a most perfect combination. Here within sound of the sea, sheltered by the pines and cooled by mellowed ocean breezes, one forgets there is a world of activity in the borders beyond."

Right:
Husband and wife vaudeville team, Charlie Ross and Mabel Fenton, hug each other in a spoof of "Antony & Cleopatra" for the photograph on this Rotograph series postcard c.1905. The celebrated couple lived at their "farm" on Deal Lake, Wanamassa, where they ran a restaurant with entertainment.

ROSS & FENTON

The Eclectic Life

In earlier days, the talented couple had "trod the boards" as they toured the country. Born in 1859, Charlie Ross, whose real name was Charles J. Kelly, started as a horseback rider in the Barnum and Bailey Circus. While touring in the West, he met performer Mabel Fenton (her real name was Ada Towne) and they married in 1887. The couple joined the popular Weber & Fields team when they opened their New York music hall in 1895 and they worked together until 1904. During that period, they discovered the "farm."

The Ross-Fenton Farm, Deal Lake, Asbury Park, N. J.

This view of the Ross-Fenton Farm published by Arthur Livingston c.1906 features one of the resort's excursion boats, "The Fenton" that would take guests to the bungalows and restaurant on "Deal Lake, Asbury Park" (Wanamassa). Postcards of the lake and farm from various angles are extremely plentiful.

Although they kept rustic Adirondack style furniture outdoors, the interior of the main house at "the farm" reflected more elaborate décor. Ross and Fenton had accumulated a collection of "heirlooms, and costly curios and bric-a-brac" and fine furnishings. A professional decorator who lived in nearby Interlaken, Charles Ables, worked with Ross to decorate the house. Besides antiques, Charlie and Mabel kept a good stock of fine wines, liquors, and plenty of expensive champagne at "the farm." The eclectic blend of country and city, rustic and elegant, was part of the magic at the Ross-Fenton farm.

A Robbery

The year 1902 brought some difficulties for Ross and Fenton. In March, *The Trenton Times* reported that Mabel was robbed by highwaymen on her way home to the farm after leaving the North Asbury Park railroad station. As she was riding in a wagon, two men jumped out from the bushes, one grabbing the horse by the bridle and the other trying to jump in with the horrified actress. The driver bravely fought off the attackers with his buggy whip. Then he sped on, but the robbers had snatched Fenton's valise containing one of her best dresses and other expensive items. The suitcase was later retrieved, however, as the gallant driver went back for it and fought the men once again. He was slightly injured.

A rarely seen photo of Charlie Ross and Mabel Fenton by their bungalow at The Ross-Fenton farm in Wanamassa has been enlarged from a montage of pictures depicting the actors' resort complex that appeared in a 1910 promotional booklet for Asbury Park.

A Raging Fire

While Ross and Fenton were in Providence, Rhode Island, a fire broke out at the New Jersey farm on October 29, 1902. The couple was temporarily renting their Jersey shore resort to Charles W. Smith, a caterer from Philadelphia, with the intention of taking it over again as soon as Smith's lease ran out. The fire started shortly before 10 pm in the Dutch kitchen that had a huge open fireplace. The employees first thought they could contain it, but the blaze got worse. Finally, they called the Asbury Park Fire Department. It was difficult for them to get their apparatus down the steep roadway to the lake, where they hoped to get sufficient water to fight the fire. The water was very shallow and full of dead leaves, so the fire fighters dug a hole in the bottom of the lake in an attempt to pump water out.

Champagne Flowed Like Water

Meanwhile, the staff began to remove items from the burning house. According to the *Asbury Park Press*, the first place they emptied was the café where hundreds of bottles of vintage champagne were rescued from the cellar and hidden in places about the trunks of the trees. "The saying that champagne flowed like water was true last night if it ever was. In fact there was more champagne than there was water, and nearly everybody who left the premises carried away from a pint to five quarts of it." Resident tenant Smith seemed crazed at the loss and cried while he watched the destruction of the building. He told the firemen they might as well help themselves to the booze, rather than let it be destroyed.

Besides the bottles, firemen did manage to save some furniture, a good piano, some knick knacks, and silverware, but most of the Ross-Fenton treasures and irreplaceable heirlooms were lost. Fortunately, no one was injured, but the building was declared a total loss. Ross and Fenton had insurance and decided to rebuild. The new farm became even more popular than the old one.

By the Light of the Silvery Moon

Of course, Ross & Fenton personally knew many top entertainers who came to perform at their lakeside resort. The stars reputed to have appeared in the early years included Lillian Russell, Marie

Dressler, Irish tenor John McCormack, Fay Templeton, and Bessie Clayton. Well-known bands played 'til all hours of the morning. Local residents, who might not have been able to afford an evening at the farm, would paddle canoes in the lake close to the Farm in order to enjoy the moonlight and to listen to the music and entertainment from the water. What a romantic and inexpensive way to spend an evening! The only drawback might have been some itchy bug bites, but Ross claimed that, "the much talked of Jersey mosquito is unknown for the restless running water of Deal Lake affords him no resting place."

The Curtain Closes

After Charles Ross died in 1918, Mabel was left to run "The Farm," which was a hot spot during Prohibition (1920-1933). But in the early 1920s, Mabel leased the place to Mr. Albright, President of the Rubberset Company. Frank Ford, a Newark restaurateur, became the new manager. Gourmet meals prepared by French chefs were on the menu in the "Wisteria Room" or on the Terrace.

Ross-Fenton Farm, Deal Lake, Asbury Park, N. J.

A postcard of the Ross-Fenton Farm postmarked 1936 shows a new dock and boathouse with characteristics of a pagoda on Deal Lake. It's quite a different-looking scene from the earlier views.

"Afternoon tea" was featured, but illegal liquor and gambling undoubtedly attracted a larger number of the clientele. Big name entertainers appeared at the farm every weekend. In the early 1930s, such legendary stars as Sophie Tucker and Ethel Merman made appearances. A popular story describes how singer Helen Morgan arrived by seaplane to do a midnight show. Residents of the area were provided with torches and stood around the banks of Deal Lake and on the Sunset Avenue Bridge to light up the landing area for Morgan's safe landing.

Mabel's health deteriorated and in 1926 she moved to California, where she died in 1931. In 1943, the Township of Ocean foreclosed on the property. The main house burned again in 1950, this time not to be replaced as a restaurant and nightclub. Theater exhibitor Walter Reade Jr. brought the farm for a cottage development and houses were built on the property, which extended from Wicapecko Drive to the lake, and from South Wanamassa Drive to Wardell Place.

Mabel Fenton and Charles Ross are buried in Glenwood Cemetery in West Long Branch. A prominent gravestone displays the names of the two stars who made their "farm" at Wanamassa a fabled place.

A Diva's Hideaway at Deal – Lillian Nordica

"If I thought I could help the cause of woman's suffrage by going out and throwing a brick through a window or adopting any other militant tactics, I would do it, but I believe in a woman being feminine and making herself as attractive as possible. By always looking her best, she gains more points. And I do not approve mannish dress."[1] Madame Lillian Nordica, 1913

Opera star Lillian Nordica always dressed well and liked her surroundings to be as elegant as her appearance. The outside of "The Nordica Bungalow" at Deal looked like an Adirondack-style log cabin, but the interior décor reflected the European tastes of its namesake. The spacious cabin's furnishings included Oriental rugs, medieval tapestries, porcelain vases, leather-bound classics, exquisite Tiffany lamps, and plenty of potted palms. The New Jersey shore home was a wedding present from her adoring third husband, banker George W. Young.

A rare c.1910 photo of the American opera star Lillian Nordica and her husband George W. Young in their Deal Adirondack-style cabin with its incongruous plush interior. The "love nest" that Young built for Nordica was off Roseld Avenue on the grounds of what is now The Hollywood Golf Club. Schnitzspahn/Moss Archives.

This photo-graph shows the exterior of the Nordica bungalow, an Adirondack style cabin at Deal, c.1910. Moss Archives.

A Soprano is Born

The stunning prima donna, Madame Nordica, did not come from Europe. She was born Lillian Norton in rural Farmington, Maine, in 1857, and moved to Boston when she was only seven. In 1868, she was inspired to sing after her entire family attended a Boston performance of the great opera star, Parepa-Rosa. Lillian studied at the New England Conservatory and her first public appearance was as a soprano soloist at Grace Church, Boston. Around 1878, Lillian Norton toured Europe and studied at Milan where her teacher gave her the stage name, Madame Nordica. She gained great popularity at the best opera houses in Europe.

In 1881, while making her debut at the Grand Opera in Paris, she met an American reporter and inventor named Frederic A. Gower, who was a distant cousin of hers from Maine. She married him two years later. At that time, Gower was working as business manager for Alexander Graham Bell promoting Bell's exciting innovation, the telephone.

Right:
Madame Lillian Nordica as Brunnhilde. A postcard published in Germany c.1910, depicts the world famous American diva who once lived at Deal in one of her most famous operatic roles.

Lillian Nordica
(as Brünnhilde)

Lost While Ballooning

It quickly became apparent that the marriage was not working out. In 1886, while Nordica had a lawsuit pending against him, Gower disappeared while crossing the English Channel in a balloon. His body was never found and his disappearance remains a mystery. Apparently, the marriage was considered to be over and Nordica went on to become a great success back in the United States. In 1896, she married a Hungarian tenor, Zoltan F. Dome, but once again marriage didn't work, and she divorced him in 1904.

The Diva Sells Soft Drinks

Lillian continued with her operatic career and posed for Coca-Cola™ advertisements and promotional merchandise from 1903 to 1905. Her image appeared on serving trays, posters, signs, sampling coupons, bookmarks, and calendars.

This metal tray features prima donna Lillian Nordica holding a huge feather fan in 1902. It is an inexpensive reproduction made to commemorate the Coca-Cola™ Bottling Company's 75th Anniversary (1902-1977). In a 2000 internet auction, bids for an original Nordica celluloid Coca-Cola™ sign featuring Nordica went over $ 20,000.

Finding Love at Fifty

When the news broke in 1908 that Madame Nordica, now almost fifty, was engaged to wealthy New Jersey financier George W. Young, the press went wild and the public devoured the story. Nordica and Young tried to rebuff the rumors of their plans, but they were married in London in July of 1909.

The great diva's husband was born George Washington Young, in 1864, in Jersey City. There he worked his way from office boy to bank executive while still in his twenties. He held several railroad directorships and owned homes in Irvington, New Jersey; in New York City; and property at the New Jersey shore. He had been married and had two children, but he received an uncontested divorce in 1908, the year before he married Madame Nordica.

On the Links

George Young had speculated in real estate, and in 1895 he purchased land along Roseld Avenue, in Deal, Ocean Township. Along with a partner, J. Henry Haggerty, he established the first golf course at the New Jersey shore, a nine-hole course designed by Lawrence Van Etten. After using the course for three years, Young formally established the Deal Golf Club in 1898, and served as its president from 1900 through 1906. Soon after the turn of the century, he acquired another 155 acres off Roseld Avenue in the West Deal section, closer to Norwood Avenue, where he erected a luxurious building called Oakwood Hall, with carriage houses and a swimming pool.

A Party to Remember

In 1909, Young had a rustic bungalow and a small building to be used as a rehearsal hall built for his adored new wife as her wedding gift. The bungalow was on the western end of his property, where he had plans to construct another golf course. On June 28, 1910, George Young threw a grand house-warming party on the lawn of the bungalow for hundreds of well-heeled guests, many of them arriving from New York on a specially chartered train. The approximately four-hundred party-goers were entertained by an orchestra and members of the Russian ballet.

In the Name of Charity

Nordica enjoyed luxury, but she also contributed to charities and worked for causes, including women's suffrage. Although she was against militancy, she campaigned for the cause of women's rights. During her time at the Deal bungalow, she reportedly attended The Wayside Methodist Church in Oakhurst and donated carpeting for the church and shrubbery for the grounds.

Within a few years, the Youngs' marriage started to fall apart, despite Lillian advancing George $400,000 to stay solvent in the face of financial problems. In 1912, he was leasing the golf course and Oakwood Hall to the recently incorporated Deal Golf Club, and his 150-acre estate including the "Nordica bungalow" to the Hollywood Golf Club, that was previously in West Long Branch. In the Fall of 1913, Young ended up having to sell the properties.

Shipwrecked in the Pacific

Nordica had given up touring, but she became restless and wanted to go on the road again. In April of 1913, she set off (with her troupe but not her husband) on a "farewell" tour of the world. The diva was apparently planning to make her way from New York westward around the world to England, where she would meet George Young. But she became ill after the Dutch steamer Tasman, on which she and her troupe were traveling, ran aground on a remote Pacific island near New Guinea. Suffering from nervous prostration and later from pneumonia, she had insisted that she be transported to Batavia, Java, from the remote island. There she died, in May of 1914, as a result of the trauma suffered from the shipwreck.

A Change of Heart

The body of Madame Nordica, the great American prima donna, was returned to her husband, George W. Young. He also received a copy of a brand new will that she had made while traveling on the steamer. She cut him out from her fortune, that she previously had bequeathed to him. Young was devastated, as he had already suffered considerable financial loss.

George Young lived at a hotel in New York after Lillian's death, and there he suffered a stroke in early February 1926. He recuperated at his brother's home in Atlantic City, but died there a few weeks later at the age of sixty-three.

The Nordica Bungalow no longer exists as it did when the diva and Young lived there. Greatly modified and expanded, the cabin now is part of The Hollywood Golf Club that is not open to the public.

The name of the intriguing Madame Lillian Nordica is often recognized as that of a great star, even by those who never heard her sing!

Finale

"The stage is not merely the meeting place of all the arts, but is also the return of art to life." Oscar Wilde

Entertainment and Technology

By the end of the roaring twenties, as the lean years of The Great Depression set in, the nature of popular entertainment had changed. Now you could see and hear the stars on a theater screen for less money than you would pay to attend live plays. You didn't have to wait for your favorite star to stop at your town on a tour. The same was true for musical stars. You could tune in the radio or play records to hear an adored opera diva or dance to the music of your favorite band right in your own living room.

In the Garden State

New Jersey was a proving ground for inventions that would revolutionize entertainment. A Newark clergyman, Rev. Hannibal Goodwin, was responsible for developing flexible roll film in 1887. Thomas A. Edison pioneered the phonograph at Menlo Park and film making at his West Orange laboratory with his assistant William K. Dickson. Fort Lee represented the heart of the silent film industry in the early twentieth century with studios there from about 1907 to the early 1920s. Radio has origins in Monmouth County with Guglielmo Marconi's historic 1899 wireless transmission from the Twin Lights (Highlands) and his experiments at Camp Evans (Wall Township). During the 1920s, commercial radio developed rapidly. In 1921, Monmouth County's first radio station broadcasted from Red Bank.

The popularity of motion pictures was undoubtedly a major factor in the decline of live theater. Movie theaters were built and well attended even during the Great Depression. Films and recordings gave performers a certain immortality that appealed to them. Old time stage stars decided to try films, but innovations such as close ups didn't suit many of them. Newly discovered stars could become famous in films, even without previous stage experience.

Recordings gave performing artists a way to be heard by many more people. Some stage, musical, and vaudeville performers ventured into radio successfully because, of course, their voices were already well trained. Radio became a powerful medium but was overtaken by television after World War II. The technology was ever changing and remains so. Yet, even as television became common place in American homes in the 1950s, it seemed that people would still go out to a movie to see their favorite stars on the big screen.

Watching "photo plays" outdoors was all the rage at the shore in the early twentieth century. This "Airdrome," c.1914 at Ocean and Brighton Avenues in Long Branch, the former site of Phil Daly's gambling club, was showing a western, *Fight At Grizzly Gulch* and *Resurrection* with Blanche Walsh. Other Airdromes were located at Sea Bright and at Highland Beach. Although the audience sat in chairs, these might be considered forerunners of drive-in theaters. The world's first drive-in opened in Pennsauken, New Jersey in 1933. Not only are the airdromes history, but all the drive-ins in New Jersey are now closed.

Roll 'Em!

Monmouth County has a tradition of movie making. While the silent film industry was centered in Fort Lee, in northern New Jersey, some early "flickers" were shot on location in Long Branch, Asbury Park, and other shore towns. Actor and director David Wark Griffith (better known as D.W. Griffith), made movies at numerous places in New Jersey including sites around Atlantic Highlands for the Biograph Company.

In 1915, Red Bank photographer Joseph Dickoff shot silent films along Branch Avenue, Pinckney Road, and at the Fox estate in Little Silver. In 1926, Paramount-Famous Players Lasky Moving Pictures Corporation took footage of ice boats from the North Shrewsbury Ice Boat and Yacht Club for a film called Fascinating Youth.

Photographer and inventor Daniel D. Dorn started out as a projectionist for nickelodeons in Asbury Park and Bradley Beach. He filmed newsreels for Fox and later for Bamberger's news of New Jersey. Around 1916, he moved his family to Red Bank. With his son Daniel W. Dorn, he produced films in the 1930s including *Romance and Red Bank* that attracted big crowds to the Carlton Theater. Cleverly using local sites for filming and residents as his stars, he made similar "Romance" films in several Monmouth County towns as well as in several other states. Local businesses would pay for advertising in the films that did quite well despite the Depression. The Dorn family operated a photography business in downtown Red Bank from 1936 until 2005.

Although a lull in local filmmaking existed during the 1940s-1960s, it picked up again in the 1970s and 1980s. A number of major motion pictures have scenes that were filmed in Monmouth County including Woody Allen's *Stardust Memories* (1980) at Ocean Grove, *Ragtime* (1981) at Spring Lake, *Annie* (1982) at Monmouth University in West Long Branch, and *City by the Sea* (2002) with Robert DeNiro, using shots of Asbury Park including the Park (former Lyric) theater.

Red Bank has become a Mecca for young filmmakers in recent years. Famous producer, director and actor Kevin Smith was born in Red Bank in 1970, and grew up in Highlands. His ground-breaking movies include *Clerks* (1994) and *Chasing Amy*. (1997). Smith maintains an office and a comic book store in Red Bank.

Daniel D. Dorn (left) holds a megaphone while his son Daniel W. Dorn stands ready to crank the camera, c.1930. They are in the backyard of their home on Pinckney Road in Red Bank. The duo shot professional films of local scenes and people for their *"Romance in…"* series that delighted theater audiences. *Dorn's Classic Images.*

Staying Alive

Although live theater waned in the Depression Era, one bright note was the work of the New Deal's Federal Theater Project of the WPA. In the late 1930s, they brought a variety of live entertainment to the people and the Monmouth County contingent had an exceptional troupe of artists.

Eventually, the Broadway tryouts at the shore petered out as the larger theaters shut down and previews became common in various cities scattered across the country. At one time, it seemed like every shore town had a theater where vaudeville acts performed and new talent could be seen. Actor Bernard Gorcey (1886-1955), who was in the "Bowery Boys" movies with his sons Leo and David, got his start at the old Broadway Theater in Long Branch by reciting a poem at amateur night. In the northern Monmouth County town of Keyport, a young brother and sister act made their debut at a pier theater in 1905. The children's names were Fred and Adele Astaire. This launched the great career of dancer Fred Astaire, later so well known in the movies. Vaudeville and films were shown together for decades, but by the early 1950s and television, vaudeville had almost completely faded away.

From the Second World War through the 1960s, entertainment at the New Jersey Shore mostly meant boardwalk amusements and rides, and maybe a movie on a rainy day. There were night clubs and hotels with live music and some tryouts at Asbury Park, Long Branch, and Atlantic City. Some professional repertory and dance companies performed, but the interest in live theater was nothing like that of the previous generations.

Nevertheless, amateur theatrical groups, schools and university drama departments, religious and other organizations offered live performances that helped to keep theater viable through the years. Today, live concerts and festivals are presented at dozens of venues, big and small, at the Monmouth County Shore. Legitimate theaters are making a comeback as people find that getting out away from all the home technology is needed. DVD's and movies on laptop computers are great innovations, but are not the same as going out to a show. Participation in the group dynamics of being part of a live audience is being rediscovered.

Most of the old shore theaters and vaudeville/movie palaces are gone, some destroyed by fires and others by wrecking balls. The argument can be made that neglected theaters are far too deteriorated to save. But many preservationists, historians, and nostalgia buffs disagree.

Restorations are important, but new theaters also need to be built. Both require funding. Fortunately, thanks to the efforts of dedicated groups and individuals, a handful of old theaters are alive and well today. Also, theatrical troupes, musicians, and artists are finding homes as new venues open. There are currently several fine professional repertory theaters. The cities of Red Bank, Long Branch, Asbury Park have each been experiencing their own unique renaissance. The potential for more performance spaces all over Monmouth County is endless...

Stars of Today

The actors' colonies at the New Jersey Shore had gradually disappeared by the end of the 1920s, but in the 1980s and 1990s, a new wave of celebrities "colonized" the Monmouth County Shore. Rock superstar Bruce Springsteen set the example. Born in Long Branch in 1949 and raised in Freehold, he gained musical fame at clubs in Asbury Park in the 1970s and wrote songs featuring places in New Jersey. In 1991, Springsteen, known as "The Boss," married Monmouth County shore native Patti Scialfa, a singer who was a member of his E Street Band, and they maintain a home in Rumson.

Rock star, Jon Bon Jovi (who was born in Perth Amboy in 1962 and grew up in Sayreville, in Middlesex County) is associated with the Monmouth County shore where he resides with his family.

New Jersey-born drummer Max Weinberg was with Springsteen's former E Street Band, and more recently performs with his own band regularly on the Conan O'Brien late night television show. Weinberg and his family are well-respected residents of Monmouth County.

Several famous television journalists are former residents of Middletown Township, including Geraldo Rivera (who was an owner of *The Two River Times*), Connie Chung, and Maury Povitz, and news anchor Brian Williams.

"The Boss." Monmouth County's own Bruce Springsteen as he appeared in his "glory days" of the 1970s. The rock idol, was born in Long Branch, grew up in Freehold, and first gained fame at Asbury Park clubs. He is part of the current "colony" of stars who live in Monmouth County today.

More stars associated with the Monmouth County shore include: movie and television actor Cesar Romero (1907-1994), who lived in Bradley Beach; actor Jack Nicholson from Neptune, born in 1937, was raised by his grandparents and went to Manasquan High School; actor and producer Danny DeVito was born in Neptune in 1944, and grew up in Asbury Park where he once worked as a hairdresser; brothers Billy Van Zandt (actor, television producer and author of numerous plays with Jane Milmore of Middletown) and "Little Steven" Van Zandt (another original member of the E Street Band who acts in The Sopranos) and 1970s folk rock legend Melanie (Safka) came from Middletown Township. Actress Adrienne Barbeau, married to Billy Van Zandt, is a resident of Navesink. Movie star of the twenty-first century Kirsten Dunst was born in Point Pleasant (Ocean County) in 1982 and went to a private school in Monmouth County.

Star Gazing

This is by no means a complete list of celebrities associated with the Monmouth County shore. Towns not covered in this volume are also home to well-known performers. The roster of names keeps growing, as there are new faces in the area soon to make their mark and established stars buying houses on the New Jersey coast all the time. "Star sightings" are frequently reported at various locations…keep your eyes open!

The next time you take a stroll on a clear summer's night at the beach or boardwalk or by the riverside, you may find that after the stars have gone…they still light up the sky.

Endnotes

Act I - Long Branch
The Lure of "The Branch"
   1. The Durnell Collection, Long Branch Free Public Library.

Prince of Players – Edwin Booth
   1. Ruggles, *Prince of Players*, p. 224.
   2. Winter, *Life of Edwin Booth*, p.75
   3. Personal correspondence from Booth to Barrett, 1871, in the collection of The Hampden-Booth Theatre Library, New York, NY.
   4. Ibid.
   5. Map in "Long Branch," a complimentary souvenir book for guests, published by Leland's Ocean Hotel, 1885. Rutgers University Archives and Special Collections, Rutgers University Alexander Library, New Brunswick, NJ.
   6. Monmouth County Archives, Manalapan, NJ. DB252, pg. 149.
   7. As stated in a letter from author Gene Smith to KLS, March 27, 1993.
   8. The article says that Edwin Booth had a "villa fronting the ocean." The house, "Fairlawns," that Edwin Booth built in 1871 was set back a few miles from the ocean in the what is now Ocean Township. The mention of his oceanfront home likely refers to his brother Joe Booth's house that was on Ocean Avenue.

The Merry Cricket – Maggie Mitchell
   1. Durnell Collection, in notes by Durnell, Long Branch Public Library.
   2. *Famous American Actors of Today*, Wingate & McKay, 1896, p. 313.

3. *The Sun*, NY. March 23, 1918, obituary of Maggie Mitchell.

4. This seems to be a popular story but difficult to verify. Various individuals claim that J.W Booth had a photo of Maggie Mitchell on him at the time of his death, but no source to prove this has been located to date by this author. KLS

5. Brown, *History of the American Stage*, 1870.

6. Wingate, *Famous American Actors of Today*, p. 319.

7. Ibid., p. 320.

8. Henderson, Theatre in America, p. 126.

9. Ibid.

10. The Durnell Collection, Long Branch Free Public Library.

Family Ties – The Wallacks

1. *Entertaining A Nation*, p. 103.

2. "James Durnell, New York Realtor, Historian, Recalls Days in City," *Long Branch Daily Record*, May 5, 1964.

An Actor's Nest – Frank Chanfrau

1. "The American on the Stage," *Scribner's Monthly*, July 1879, p. 326.

The Fairy Princess - Mary Anderson

1. The Durnell Collection, Long Branch Free Public Library

2. *Norwood Park* by Fischer, states that the correct name of the Munro cottage was "Normahurst" named after his daughter Norma, not "Normanhurst."

The Jersey Lily – Lillie Langtry

1. *Entertaining A Nation*, p. 89.

2. The winery, though owned by others for many years, still honors Lillie and her California house was restored and opened as a tourist site.

Beauty and the Gourmand – Lillian Russell and Diamond Jim Brady

1. *Entertaining A Nation*, p. 120.

2. Excerpt from "A Provincial Sense of Time," an essay by Robert Pinsky, used with the author's permission.

3. "Diamond Jim Brady Buys a Farm," *The New York Times*, November 18, 1906, p. 2.

Act II - North Long Branch and Monmouth Beach
Wild West Showman – Nate Salsbury
1. The Durnell Collection, Long Branch Free Public Library.
2. Rebecca married photographer Paul Strand. "Beck" and Strand had a close relationship with artist Georgia O'Keefe and her husband, photographer Alfred Stieglitz. After her divorce from Strand, Rebecca married a man with the last name James. Rebecca Salsbury James lived in New Mexico and became a well known painter.
3. *Entertaining A Nation*, p. 115.
4. Ibid., p. 115.

A Foresighted Cottager – Oliver Byron
1.Busby, *The Oliver Byron Legacy*, 2006, p. 25.
2. Ibid., p. 25
3. Ibid., p. 10
4. *Entertaining A Nation*, p. 82
5. The Garfield Hut remained there, neglected for decades, but is now restored thanks to The Long Branch Historical Association and a grant from the Monmouth County Historical Commission.
Note: Mr. Busby's book, available from The Monmouth Beach Cultural Center, includes detailed information about all the Byron properties and a map.

Act III – Red Bank and Fair Haven
The Kid from Red Bank – Count Basie
1. *Good Morning Blues, The Autobiography of Count Basie*, p. 28.
2. The house was rebuilt in the early 1970s. There is no museum or memorial to see at the site which is private.
3. Basie referred to him as "Henry" LaRoss.
4. *Good Morning Blues, The Autobiography of Count Basie*, p. 31.
5. The Westside YMCA no longer exists, the local branches of the organization are unified and exist as "The Community YMCA" today with headquarters in Red Bank.

Fair Haven's Bohemians – The Vaudevillians

1. Information about Lockwood (Smith) is according to articles and lectures by author-historian Timothy McMahon.

2. According to Timothy McMahon in his lectures.

3. The source of this information is the club's history on the website of the current Shrewsbury River Boat Club.

Act IV – Highlands and Atlantic Highlands
A Female Impersonator – Neil Burgess

1. Highlands (The Making of America Series) by John P. King, p. 81.

The Jolly Troubadour – Nellie McHenry

1. *New York Times*, Obituary for Nellie McHenry, May 5, 1935.

2. As quoted in "Stars in the Highland Hills," by Muriel Smith, *Asbury Park Press*, May 16, 1994.

A Romantic Farmer and His Wives – Robert B. Mantell

1. Several sources state that the show was *Macbeth*, but the *Red Bank Register* from 1911 advertises that the play was *As You Like It* which is most likely correct. Marie Booth Russell was to play Rosalind, but due to her illness, Genevieve Hamper probably understudied for her.

2. A full-length biography of Genevieve Hamper by the author of this book is pending publication at the present time.

Act V - Around Asbury Park
Piety and Performance

1. *Asbury Park's Glory Days*, by Pike, p. 18.

2. Walter Rosenberg had become Walter Reade. He and his son, Walter Reade Jr., operated a movie chain "empire" with eighty theaters in ten states and headquarters in Ocean Township until the business went bankrupt in the early 1970s.

A Famous Music Maker – Arthur Pryor

1. *New York Times* 5/9/1942. Note: Ann Sothern married actor Robert Sterling the following year. Sothern is often remembered for two popular television sitcoms she starred in during the 1950s.

The Simple Life – Ross & Fenton

1. *Asbury Park - Where County Meets the Sea.* 1910 promotional book, p.35.

A Diva's Hideaway at Deal – Lillian Nordica

1."Nordica Against Militancy." *The New York Times*, March 22, 1913, p.1.

Selected Bibliography

Benjamin, Richard. "Arthur Pryor: Ragtime Pioneer." http://www.paragonragtime.com/pryor.html.

Boardman, Gerald. *The Oxford Companion to American Theatre*. New York: Oxford University Press, 1992.

Blum, Daniel. *Great Stars of the American Stage, A Pictorial Record*: New York, Grosset & Dunlap, 1952.

Brown, T. Allston. *History of the American Stage*: New York: Dick & Fitzgerald, Publishers, 1870.

Bulliet, C.J. *Robert Mantell's Romance*. Boston: John W. Luce & Company, 1918.

Busby, William J. *The Oliver Byron Legacy, Showman and Builder*. North Long Branch, NJ: W.J. Busby, 2006.

Carlyon, David. *Dan Rice, The Most Famous Man You've Never Heard Of*. New York: Public Affairs, 2001.

"Cinema Treasures." http://cinematreasures.org

"Count Basie Theatre." http..countbasietheatre.org/history.php

Edelson, Marjoire and Zimmerer, Kay. *Township of Ocean*. Dover, NH: Arcadia Publishing, 1997.

Fischer, Robert J. *Norwood Park, An Exclusive Summer Cottage Colony*. NJ: West Long Branch Historical Society, Inc., 2000.

Gabrielan, Randall, *Fair Haven*. Dover, NH: Arcadia Publishing, 1997.

_____, *Fair Haven, The Making of an American Town*. Charleston, SC: Arcadia Publishing, 1998.

_____, *Long Branch People and Places*. Charleston, SC: Arcadia Publishing, 1998.

_____, *Monmouth Beach and Sea Bright*. Dover, NH: Arcadia Publishing, 1998.

_____, *Red Bank*. Dover, NH: Arcadia Publishing, 1995.

_____, *Red Bank, Vol. II*. Dover, NH: Arcadia Publishing, 1996.

_____, *Red Bank, Vol. III*. Charleston, SC: Arcadia Publishing, 1998.

Glackens, Ira. *Yankee Diva, Lillian Nordica and the Golden Days of Opera*. New York: Coleridge Press, 1963.

Grossman, Edwina Booth. *Edwin Booth, Recollections by His Daughter and Letters to Her and To His Friends*. New York: The Century Co., 1902.

Henderson, Mary C. *Theatre in America*. New York: Harry N. Abrams, Inc., 1986.

"Internet Broadway Database." http://www.ibdb.com/

"Internet Movie Database." http://www.imdb.com/

Jeffers, H. Paul. *Diamond Jim Brady, Prince of the Gilded Age*. New York: John Wiley & Sons, Inc., 2001.

Kiernan, Mary Ann. *The Monmouth Patent, Part I*. Red Bank, New Jersey: The Greater Red Bank Voice, 1986.

King, John P. *Highlands, New Jersey, "Making of America Series,"* Charleston, SC: Arcadia, 2001.

Lucia, Peter. "The Website of Peter Lucia." http:// www.nowever-then.com.

Lurie, Maxine N. and Mappen, Marc, eds. *Encyclopedia of New Jersey*. New Brunswick, New Jersey: Rutgers University Press, 2004.

McArthur, Benjamin, *Actors and American Culture, 1880-1920*. Iowa City: University of Iowa Press, 2000.

McMahon, Timothy. *The Golden Age of the Monmouth County Shore, 1864-1914*. Fair Haven, NJ: T.J. McMahon, 1964.

Methot, June. *Up and Down the River*. Navesink, NJ: Whip Publishers, 1980.

Maps, Charles and Van Benthuysen, Robert F., eds. *The Early History of West Long Branch*. West Long Branch Historical Society, 1977.

Morrell, Parker. *Diamond Jim, the Life and Times of James Buchanan Brady*. Garden City, NY: Garden City Publishing Company, Inc., 1934.

Moss, George H. Jr. *Double Exposure Two*. Sea Bright. NJ: Ploughshare Press, 1995.

_____. *Twice Told Tales*. Sea Bright, N J: Ploughshare Press, 2002.

_____, and Schnitzspahn, Karen L. *Victorian Summers at the Grand*

Hotels of Long Branch. Sea Bright, NJ: Ploughshare Press, 2000.

Murray, Albert. *Good Morning Blues, The Autobiography of Count Basie (as told to Albert Murray)*. New York: Random House, 1985.

Phillips, Helen C. *Red Bank on the Navesink*, Red Bank, NJ: Caesarea Press, 1977.

Pike, Helen-Chantal. *Asbury Park's Glory Days*. New Brunswick, NJ: Rutgers University Press, 2005.

_____. *West Long Branch*. Dover, NH: Arcadia Publishing, 1996.

The Ross-Fenton Farm, a booklet published by The Township of Ocean Historical Museum, 1991.

Ruggles, Eleanor. *Prince of Players, Edwin Booth*. New York: W.W. Norton & Co., 1953.

Schenck, J.H, *Album of Long Branch: A Series of Photographic Views with Letter Press Sketches*. New York: John F. Trow, 1868.

"Shrewsbury River Yacht Club." http:// www.sryc.net/about.htm

Smith, Gene. *American Gothic*. New York: Simon & Schuster, 1992.

Smith, Muriel, "Stars in the Highlands Hills," *Asbury Park Press*, May 16, 1994.

Sylvester, Marie A. *Around Deal Lake*. Dover, NH: Arcadia Publishing, 1998.

Taubman, Howard. *The Making of the American Theatre*. New York: Howard-McCann, Inc., 1965.

Tobin, Brendan P. *Hollywood NJ, The Amazing Connection between Hollywood and New Jersey*. Bridgewater, NJ: Replica Books, 2005.

The Township of Ocean, Monmouth County, NJ, Commemorative Book, published for the Centennial Celebration, August 1949.

Uminowicz, Glenn, "Sport in a Middle-Class Utopia, Asbury Park, NJ, 1871-1895," *Journal of Sport History*, Vol. 11, No. 1, Spring 1984.

Wingate, Charles E.L. and McKay, F.E., eds. *Famous American Actors of Today*. Boston: Thomas Y. Crowell & Company, Boston, 1896.

Winter, William. *The Life and Art of Edwin Booth*. New York: Macmillan & Co., 1893.

Wolff, Daniel. *Fourth of July, Asbury Park*. New York and London: Bloomsbury Publishing, 2005.

Works Progress Administration. *Entertaining A Nation: The Career of Long Branch*. 1940.

York, Hildreth and Murrin, Mary R. *The Arts and Entertainment in New Jersey.* Trenton, NJ: New Jersey Historical Commission, Department of State, History Series 7, 1996.

Selected Periodicals
Asbury Park Press
Asbury Park Evening Press
Long Branch Daily Record
The Atlanticville
The Hub
The New York Dramatic Mirror
The New York Times
The Red Bank Register
The Star Ledger
The Theatre
The Trenton Times
The Two River Times
Trenton Evening Times

Other Sources:
The Durnell Collection at the Long Branch Free Public Library is an extensive archive about Long Branch history that includes many notes, photographs, programs, and clippings about theatrical people who came to Long Branch.

Deeds and building contracts, and other documents, Monmouth County Archives, Manalapan, NJ.

Miscellaneous promotional and souvenir booklets and programs.

Personal correspondence from Peggy Hollingsworth, granddaughter of Robert B. Mantell, to the author in the 1990s.

Index